ALSO BY HEALTH FOR LIFE

Amino Acids and Other Ergogenic Aids

The Back Relief Book — *A Synergistic Program for Relieving or Preventing Low Back Pain*

Explosive Power — *Plyometrics for Bodybuilders, Martial Artists & Other Athletes*

Fast on Your Feet — *Building Athletic Footspeed and Agility*

The Health For Life Training Advisor

The Human Fuel Cookbook — *Recipes for Peak Athletic Performance*

The Human Fuel Handbook — *Nutrition for Peak Athletic Performance*

Maximum Calves

Max O_2 — *The Complete Guide to Synergistic Aerobic Training*

Mind Gains — *A Synergistic Mental Focus Program for Peak Physical Performance*

Minimizing Reflex and Reaction Time

Power Forearms!

The 7-Minute Rotator Cuff Solution — *A Complete Program to Prevent & Rehabilitate Rotator Cuff Injuries*

Secrets of Advanced Bodybuilders

Secrets Supplement #1

Secrets Update

SynerShape — *A Scientific Weight-Loss Guide*

SynerStretch — *For Total-Body Flexibility*

T.N.T. — *Total Neck & Traps*

Transfigure I — *9 Minutes to the Ultimate Buttocks and Thighs*

Transfigure II — *For the Ultimate Upper Body*

The Weightless Workout — *For the Ultimate High-Intensity Bodyweight Workout Anywhere!*

ISBN 0-944831-40-0

Library of Congress Catalog Card Number: 97-075305

HEALTH FOR LIFE

8033 Sunset Blvd., Suite 483–Los Angeles, CA 90046–5622 (800) 874-5339

1 2 3 4 5 6 7 8 9

LEGENDARY ABS

Gold Edition

CREDITS AND ACKNOWLEDGMENTS

Original Legendary Abs Program by Jerry Robinson

Editor

Robert Miller

Technical Advisors

Jerry Robinson
Mark Hoffman
Eric Strernlicht, Ph.D

Additional Material

Robert Miller
Ed Derse

Book Design

Jerry Graves Design

Illustrations

Irene Di Conte
John Quinn III

Photography

Michael Neveux

Production

Maritta Tapanainen

Thanks to Eliza Lewin and Ruth Silverman for additional production support.

WARNING

LEGENDARY ABS

By Jerry Robinson & Robert Miller

Gold Edition

A SYNERGISTIC WORKOUT FOR THE ABDOMINAL MUSCLES

Contents

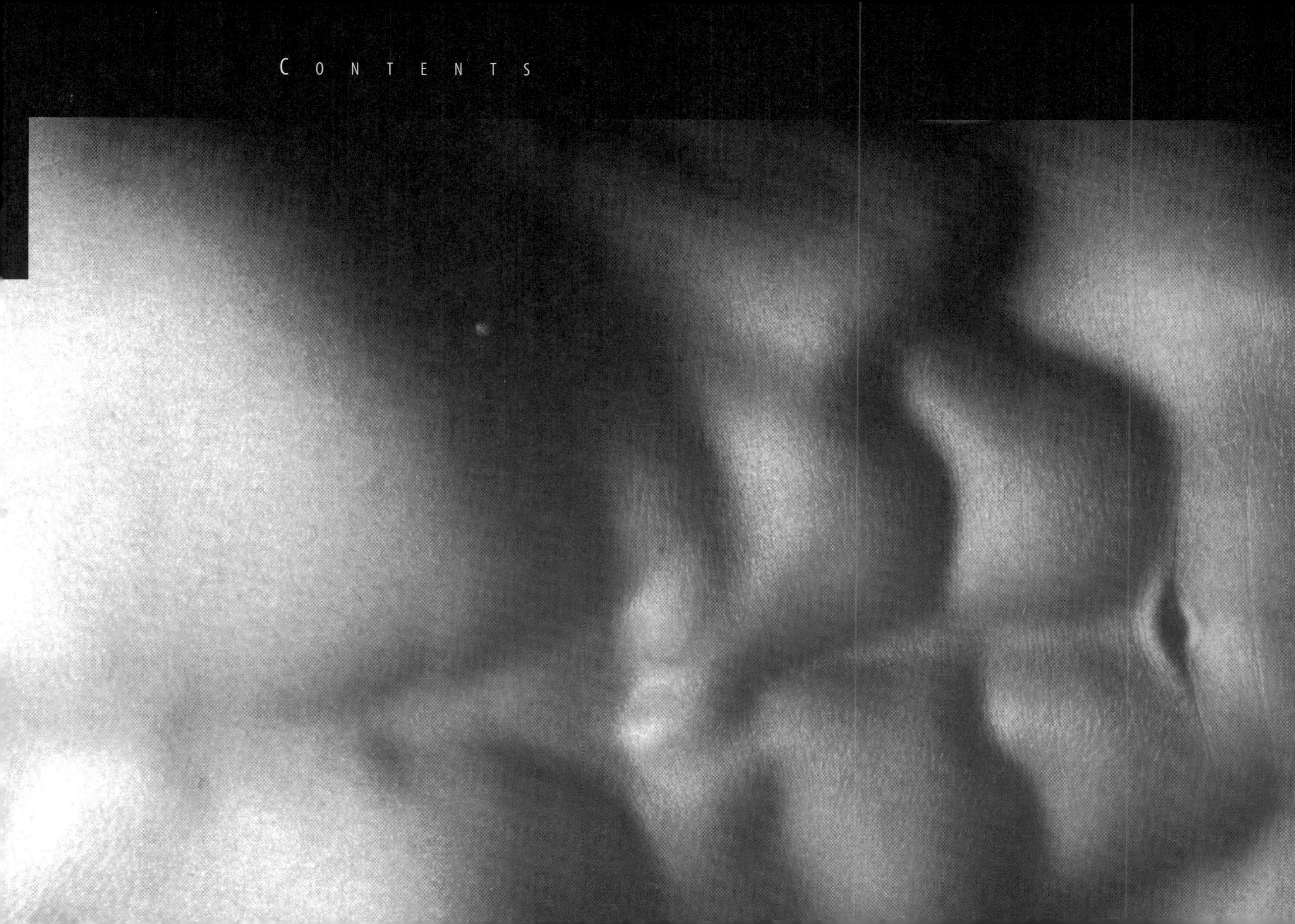
CONTENTS

Introduction

From the hundreds of letters our readers send us, it's clear that *everyone* wants great abs. People of all ages, at all levels of physical conditioning, men and women alike...a firm, flat, midsection is everyone's #1 goal!

Since its release in 1981, *Legendary Abs* has offered the fastest way to blast your abs, giving even first-time users an unbelievable burn in less than 6 minutes a workout. Over the years, we've refined the program, releasing new editions along the way. And, all along the way, customers have continued to praise it for its simplicity and effectiveness. *U.S. News & World Report* called it "The best overall stomach trimmer...."

Now we've taken our basic program a step further.

Legendary Abs "Goes Gold"

The new edition is actually *three* times as legendary as the original!

To start with, we've polished the text of the original program, clearing up certain questions raised by our readers and reconciling some inconsistencies created by years of revision. The new *Legendary Abs* is streamlined for maximum readability and and guaranteed to produce the same great results as ever.

But now there's more.

The *Gold Edition* also incorporates the complete text of *Beyond Legendary Abs*, our more technical **performance guide.** We've kept it in a separate chapter so you can decide just how in-depth you want to go.

Plus, you'll find a new ab training program **especially for athletes.** If you're looking for great performance as well as great looks, you'll find exercises and routines to increase trunk strength and stability for all athletic activities involving mid-body power and rotation.

And finally, there's a brand new section on **fat loss for abdominal definition.** After all, no one can appreciate those rock-hard abs if they're hidden under a layer of babyfat. The new *Legendary Abs* High-Low Nutritional Plan will show you how to take advantage of a never-before published technique for creating a calorie deficit without the pitfalls of standard dieting.

The new *Legendary Abs Gold Edition* gives you everything you need for every possible abdominal training goal!

A Special Note to First-Time Readers

We know a lot of you are longtime HFL customers who've purchased the *Gold Edition* for the new material it contains. But if you're just picking up this program for the first time, you probably have a few basic questions, such as...

WHAT *IS* LEGENDARY ABS?

The *Legendary Abs* program for abdominal development is the result of four years' research at Stanford University. A research team led by HFL founder Jerry Robinson studied hundreds of bodybuilders, gymnasts, martial artists, and wrestlers to learn how these athletes trained their abdominals. The researchers also reviewed the findings of numerous physiology and biomechanics studies on ab training. They used all this information to create the first edition of the *Legendary Abs* program, published in 1981.

Today, more than a million people around the world are using *Legendary Abs.* And now *you're* going to experience it for yourself.

HOW EFFECTIVE IS IT?

So effective that 95% of all beginners develop improved muscle tone in the first two weeks. Even bodybuilders are able to develop and maintain extreme definition by doing these exercises for just 6 minutes, 4 times a week! We guarantee you'll feel the power from your very first workout.

WHAT DO I HAVE TO DO?

If you want to get started as quickly as possible, just read *Chapter 1: What Makes Legendary Abs*—it will give you the basic theory behind the program. At that point, you can skip straight to Chapter 3, learn the exercises, and get down to work.

On the other hand, if you'd like to expand your understanding of the technical points, read through *Chapter 2: Beyond Legendary Abs.* This will give you additional insight into the anatomy and workings of the muscles and will improve your mental focus during your workout.

One note: You may already be familiar with some of the exercises. But the exercises alone are not what make *Legendary Abs* so effective. The real power comes from the way the exercises are combined in the routines. *It is the sequence, timing, and overall progression that make this program work.* If you are already doing some of these exercises, you'll be amazed at how much more effective they become when you do them exactly as indicated in the *Legendary Abs* routines.

Are you ready to experience the ultimate abdominal workout? Let's get started!

What's Coming Up

Chapter 1: What Makes *Legendary Abs*—An explanation of the theory behind *Legendary Abs.* Beginners should start here.

Chapter 2: Beyond *Legendary Abs*—Master the subtleties! Anatomy, muscle function, targeting, mental focus, training goals, and other topics from the first chapter are discussed in greater depth.

Chapter 3: *Legendary Abs* Basic Program—The exercises, routines, and schedule.

Chapter 4: Fat Reduction for Abdominal Definition—A complete program of aerobic exercise and dietary modification to help you lose fat and improve abdominal definition, including a unique approach to calorie restriction that avoids the metabolic slowdown caused by dieting!

Chapter 5: Training for Athletic Power—A variation of the basic abs program with additional exercises designed to increase trunk strength and stability for athletic activity.

Chapter 6: *Legendary Abs* Athletic Power Program—Exercises, routines, and schedule for building athletic power.

Appendices: Often-Asked Questions, Self Evaluation

INTRODUCTION

What Makes Legendary Abs

It's incredible how *wrong* accepted "training wisdom" can be. Did you know, for example, that the Straight-Legged Sit-Up is *not* an efficient ab exercise—and that it can even be dangerous? While the general level of knowledge on this subject is much higher than it was in 1981 when *Legendary Abs* first came out, the fact is, there's still a lot of misunderstanding about ab training. This chapter will explain what makes a good ab exercise, and how the *Legendary Abs* program works to give you phenomenal muscular development in *only 6 minutes a session.*

1

WHAT MAKES LEGENDARY ABS

A Scientific Foundation

If you want to get the most from any training program, it helps to know a few basic principles of **biomechanics**, the science of human movement. Using these principles, you can quickly tell effective, safe exercises from ineffective, potentially injurious ones and determine how best to structure your exercise routine.

This scientific foundation is what separates *Legendary Abs* from other abdominal conditioning methods. It's also what makes it possible to build great-looking abs in only 6 minutes a session.

What makes legendary abs? They're not just the result of the muscle you have—they're also the result of the fat you *don't* have. So let's start by distinguishing between **fat reduction** and **muscle conditioning** and then explore how—and how *not*—to train the abs for maximum results in minimum time.

Muscle

Muscle tissue has a very special characteristic: the ability to *contract.* When stimulated by the central nervous system, muscle fibers shorten to about two-thirds their length. Thanks to the clever way those fibers are arranged, humans can do amazing things, like run 4-minute miles, scale mountains, and perform delicate surgical procedures.

The abs in particular, besides enabling movements of the torso, help protect the body. Running from the bottom of your ribs to the top of the pubic bone, the abs serve two main purposes:

- They allow you to move your upper body in relation to your pelvis and legs, and *vice versa.*
- They shield the internal organs of the abdomen.

The abs are also essential to good posture. Together with the **spinal erector** muscles in your back, they work to keep your spine upright—much like the guy-wires supporting opposite sides of a tent pole.

At least, that's what they're designed to do.

Soft, out-of-shape abs do little supporting or protecting—nor do they add much to your appearance. That's why doing abdominal exercise is so important. Even a few minutes of ab training every week with *Legendary Abs* will make you feel stronger, healthier, and more physically secure—and, perhaps most important, it will make you look fantastic!

When it comes to appearance, however, the problem many of us have is not just out-of-shape abdominals. More often, the bigger culprit is *fat.*

Fat

Fat and muscle are two distinct and separate types of tissue. In the abdominal region, as in all areas of the body, a layer of fat covers the muscles (Fig. 1-1). The thicker this fat layer, the harder it is to see your abs no matter *how* well developed they are.

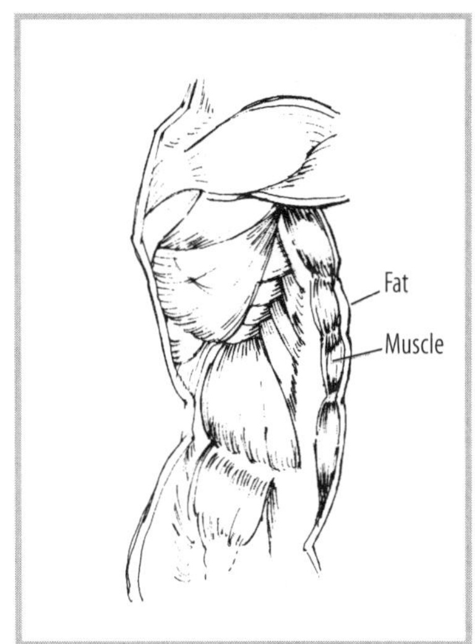

Fig. 1-1 A layer of fat covers the abs

Getting rid of unwanted fat, if that is your goal, is basically a matter of adjusting your diet and activity levels until you are using more calories than you consume (creating what's called a **calorie deficit**).

This is advice most people know and few follow! Still, it's the simple truth. Doing muscular work requires energy; your body draws that energy from the food you eat and from your fat stores. If you decrease your food intake and increase your energy output, you'll lose fat.

SPOT REDUCING

Many people mistakenly believe they can burn away abdominal fat by doing ab exercises, such as Sit-Ups or Side Bends. Unfortunately, so-called **spot reducing** doesn't work. The

reason is that abdominal exercises don't burn enough calories to create a calorie deficit. Furthermore, when fat does come off, it comes off *all over* the body—not just from the area being worked.

To get rid of excess fat, regardless of where on your body it is, you must do exercises involving as many major muscle groups as possible—exercises like running, swimming, cycling, stair climbing, or jumping rope—and you must do them consistently over a period of time. *(See Chapter 4 for specific fat-loss guidelines.)*

Legendary Abs will start to firm and tone your abdominal muscles immediately. The more you can reduce any excess stomach fat through diet and aerobic exercise, the better you'll be able to *see* the results of your *Legendary Abs* workout.

Conditioning Abdominal Muscle

To be effective, an abdominal training routine must:

- **target the abs**—The abs must be the main muscles responsible for the movements.
- **overload the abs**—The exercises must force the abs to do more work than they're used to.
- **work the abs from several angles**—The exercises must involve the greatest possible number of muscle fibers.

Many traditional abs exercises don't meet these requirements.

THE GOOD NEWS ABOUT SIT-UPS: *DON'T DO THEM!*

Two of the most common abs exercises are the Straight-Legged Sit-Up, performed lying on your back with the feet held to the floor, and the Roman Chair Sit-Up, which uses a special bench found in most gyms (Fig. 1-2).

At first glance, these seem to satisfy the first requirement on our list—that is, they seem to target the abs. After all, both movements center around the waist and cause the abdominal muscles to "burn."

But remember that a well-targeted exercise is one in which the target muscle is the *main* muscle causing the motion. That isn't the case with either of these exercises.

The fact is, the abdominals have a much narrower **range of motion** than either of these types of Sit-Ups requires. Fully two-thirds of the Straight-Legged Sit-Up is the work of muscles other than the abs. Worse yet, the Roman Chair Sit-Up has almost *no* direct ab involvement—the abs merely stabilize the body while other muscles are used to raise and lower the torso (Fig. 1-2).

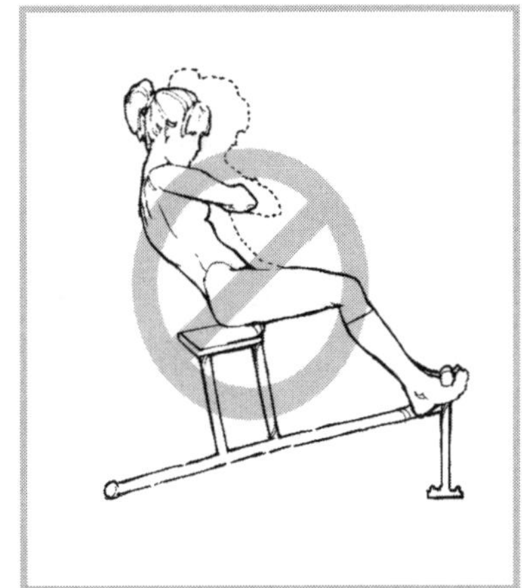

Fig. 1-2 Roman Chair Sit-Ups

Here's the rule to remember: When you're lying on your back with your legs extended, *your abs have the capacity to raise your shoulders about 30 degrees off the floor.* No further. Any exercise that involves movement beyond that is working muscles other than the abs.

Is it necessarily bad to involve other muscles? In this case, yes.

Those "other muscles" are called the psoas muscles. They run from the front of your upper leg, through the pelvis, attaching to the lower six vertebrae of your spine (Fig. 1-3). When they contract, they pull your upper body toward your legs—just as your abs do. But unlike the abs, the psoas muscles have a huge range: they can flex your body forward all the way from a full back bend until your chest touches your knees.

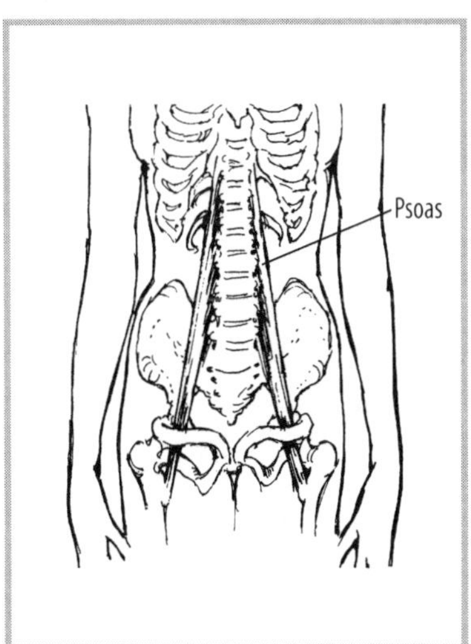

Fig. 1-3 The psoas muscles

The two psoas muscles work best when your legs are extended and/or your feet are held—as they are in both these exercises.

When you do Sit-Ups or Roman Chair Sit-Ups, the psoas compete with your abs for the first third of the movement, and then they take over entirely for the rest. As a result, only a small amount of the work you're doing is going into conditioning your abs.

Such inefficiency makes it very hard to overload the abs. Some athletes find they must do several *hundred* Sit-Ups before they feel a burn. (As a rule, any movement you can do by the hundreds is not an efficient muscle conditioning exercise!)

Worse, though, is the risk of injury from psoas-dominated movements. With each contraction, the psoas tug at their attachment on the lower spine. That tug doesn't do much harm as long as the abs remain strong enough to prevent your back from arching. But, unfortunately, even if you're in great shape, the abs tire fairly quickly. Eventually, your back begins to arch, causing the vertebrae around the psoas attachment to grind together. After a few years of this, you may be stuck with chronic lower back pain as a result of disk degeneration.

Fortunately, there are safer and more effective exercises, which we'll cover in the Exercise section. But building an effective program doesn't stop with the choice of exercises. The construction of the exercise *routine* is equally important. And one of the most crucial factors in structuring a routine is **exercise sequence.**

Synergistic Exercise Sequence

Whenever you do several exercises for the same muscle group, you're faced with the decision of what *order* to do them in. Many people just do exercises at random. Nevertheless, research has shown that some sequences are more powerful than others. Usually, there's one particular order that's best. When done in that sequence, the exercises reinforce each other, and the whole routine becomes far more effective. This is called **synergism**, and it's the backbone of the *Legendary Abs* program.

Synergistic exercise sequence is governed by a principle called the **interdependency of muscle groups**, which refers to the ways in which muscles work together to perform movements.

Interdependency affects all parts of your workout. This is because exercises rarely involve only one muscle group. Most often, two or more muscle groups cooperate in performing a movement. The problem is that usually one of them gets tired first, forcing you to stop before the other has had a good workout.

Understanding the interdependency of the abs allows us to sequence several exercises in such a way that *all* the muscles get a good workout. Here's how:

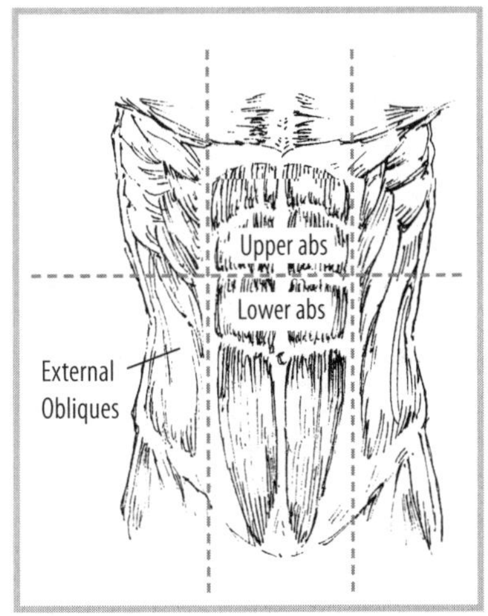

Fig. 1-4 Basic abdominal regions

First, imagine the center portion of the abdominals divided into upper and lower abdominal regions—or *upper* and *lower abs*, for short. The line is usually drawn between the top two and bottom two abdominal ridges.

The outer region of the abs we'll call by its anatomical name: the external obliques.

The upper abs and the lower abs are *interdependent* in the following way:

- When you do a *lower* ab exercise, you use both lower and upper abs.
- When you do an *upper* ab exercise, you use almost exclusively upper abs.

Notice that the upper abs play a role in working both areas. If you were to train them first, their fatigue would limit your lower ab work, preventing the lower abs from getting a good workout. The solution? Train the *lower* abs first—partially tiring the upper abs in the process—then finish off the uppers with exercises that concentrate on them.

There's a side benefit to proper sequencing: Since the uppers are partially fatigued from the lower ab work, they don't have to be pushed very hard on their own to get a good workout.

The same logic applies to training the obliques, whose job is to rotate the torso. Like the lower abs, the obliques also receive support from the upper abs. So, like the lowers, the obliques should be trained before you do any exercises aimed exclusively at the uppers.

The overall sequence of exercises should be:

- lower abs exercises
- obliques exercises
- upper abs exercises

This is the basic structure of the *Legendary Abs* routines. But it's just the beginning. Through years of experimentation, we've also determined a specific order of exercises *within* these categories, along with specific set and rep guidelines, to give you the optimum workout at each level of the program.

Putting It Together

We now have a basic strategy that conforms to our three rules of ab training.

Let's review:

Rule 1: Target the abs

Strategy: To be sure the abs are the main muscle being worked, the *Legendary Abs* program will avoid exercises that involve the psoas *and* require a body position that encourages the back to arch.

Rule 2: Overload the abs

Strategy: By keeping psoas involvement in the exercises to a minimum, you will be able to properly overload your abs.

Rule 3: Work the abs from several angles

Strategy: By taking into account the interdependency of the abdominal muscles, the *Legendary Abs* routines have been sequenced so that both upper and lower abs, and the external obliques, get a full workout.

❖ ❖ ❖

The routines in *Legendary Abs* will take you as close as you wish to the ancient Greek sculptor's idea of a well-defined midsection. The total time you'll spend on any one workout will never exceed 6 minutes.

The time it will take to reach your goal depends on your present physical condition and the consistency with which you train. It won't be long, though. If you don't have much excess fat, you should see results within a couple of weeks. Mild soreness, however, should come after the first or second workout—a definite indication that *something* good is happening!

Let's get started...

- For a more detailed look at the anatomy and function of the abs, go on to Chapter 2.
- To get started right away, skip to Chapter 3.

Beyond Legendary Abs

One of the best things about the *Legendary Abs* program is that it's really pretty foolproof. By simply following the routines, you're guaranteed a great set of abs in less than 6 minutes a session. But it's possible to get even *more* out of the program by developing your own working understanding of the concepts on which it's based.

In this chapter, we'll delve deeper into the anatomy and mechanics of the abdominals and show you how to use this information to perfect your exercise technique. You will be able to surpass previous limits—and achieve the *ultimate*, fine-tuned ab workout.

2

1+1=3

Creating a whole greater than the sum of the parts. This is **synergism.**

If you've ever watched a carpenter at work, you know that the materials most of us might use to build a simple, functional bookshelf can also be used to create a fine piece of cabinetry. Likewise, if you've ever tried to re-create a dish you enjoyed in a restaurant, you may have found that the same ingredients that make up a delicious meal can also add up to a kitchen disaster!

It's all about *design:* finding a way of arranging the parts so that they mutually reinforce and enhance each other's contribution. It's all about *synergism.*

The concept of synergism can be applied at every level of physical conditioning, from an individual rep to an overall routine—even to your life as a whole. To do this, one must continually ask: What elements are involved, and how can they best be put together?

The elements of *Legendary Abs* include muscle anatomy, exercise selection, form, focus, exercise order, timing, and schedule. These have been combined in the most synergistic way possible. Frankly, the design work's all done. You can, if you want, skip straight to the exercises and get started...

...unless you really want the *ultimate* ab workout.

The better you understand the "why" of what you're doing, the greater your potential for gains—it's that simple. This chapter will sharpen your understanding of how the abs work and how best to train them. The small refinements you'll be able to make to your exercise form and mental focus after reading this chapter can translate into major increases in training intensity.

Let's start with the muscles themselves.

The Abdominals

To isolate one muscle group and train it to the fullest, you need some basic information. Where do the muscles attach? How do they act? Along what lines of force? What other muscles support this action?

The abdominals represent one of the body's ingenious design trade-offs, addressing the need for both **protection** and **flexibility**. Clearly, the human rib cage serves the vital function of protecting the heart and lungs. Yet, if the ribs continued all the way down to the pelvis, enclosing the other organs, we'd be stuck with a skeleton that allowed very little mobility.

The abs are an elegant solution. Arranged in layers, each with fibers running in a different direction, they provide both protection and flexibility.

LOCATION AND FUNCTION

Four muscles make up the abdominal group:

- **rectus abdominis**
- **external oblique**
- **internal oblique**
- **transversalis**

Rectus Abdominis

Forming two segmented vertical bands, the *rectus abdominis* is the most prominent of the muscles. (Technically, the term *rectus abdominis* refers to two separate muscles, but they're almost always discussed collectively.) Running upward from the crest of the pubic bone, the rectus attaches to the lower ribs. When it contracts, it pulls the pelvis and the rib cage closer together (Fig. 2-1). This is called **spinal flexion**.

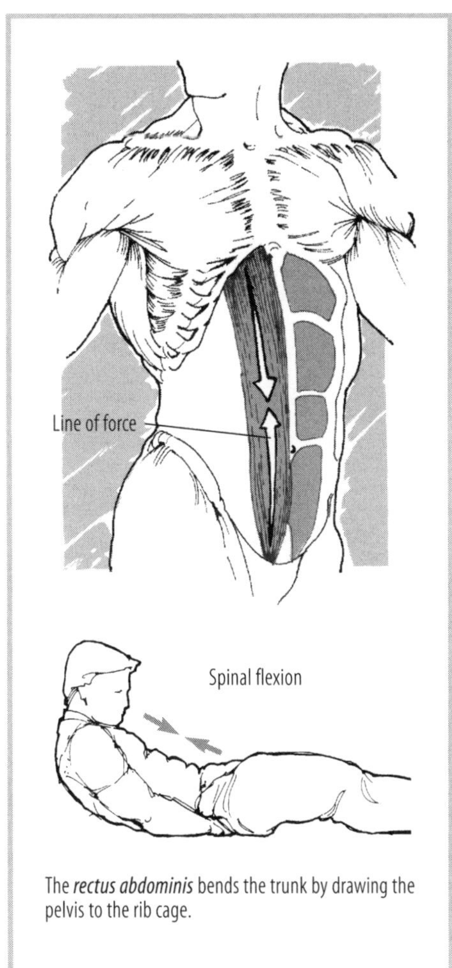

The *rectus abdominis* bends the trunk by drawing the pelvis to the rib cage.

Fig. 2-1 Rectus Abdominis

For training purposes, the rectus is divided into *upper* and *lower abs,* each composed of two pairs of "lumps."

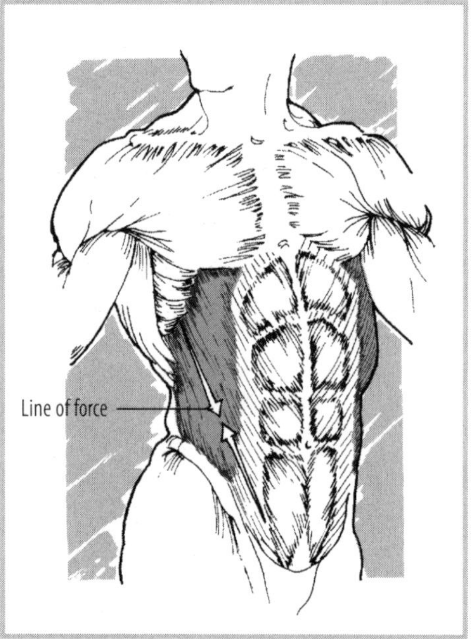

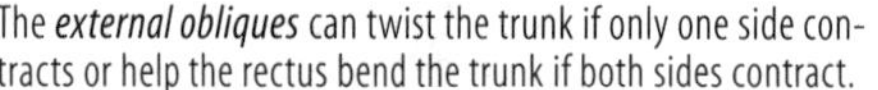
The *external obliques* can twist the trunk if only one side contracts or help the rectus bend the trunk if both sides contract.

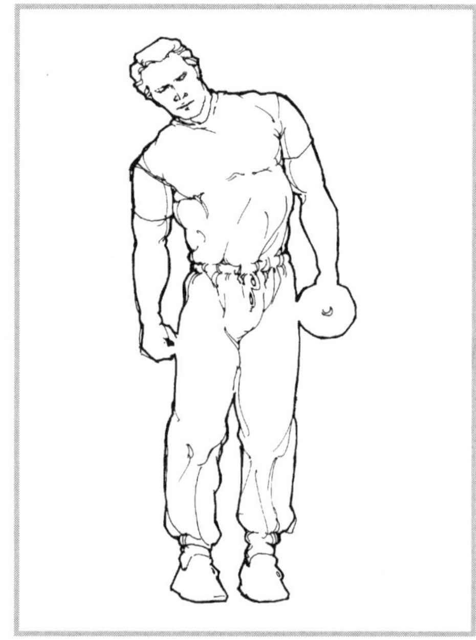

Lateral spinal flexion—one side contracting

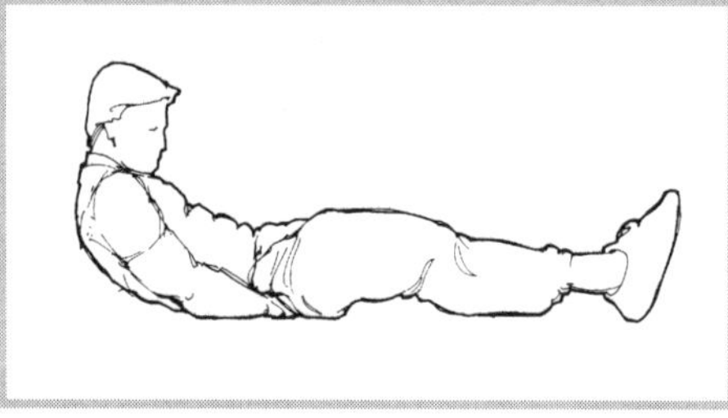

Spinal flexion—both sides contracting

Rotation—one side contracting

Fig. 2-2 External Obliques

External Obliques

The *external obliques* are two broad, flat muscles that wrap around the sides and front of the abdomen (Fig. 2-2). Their job is to stabilize the torso by resisting the rotational stresses of major body exercises. Because they run diagonally downward, a contraction of one side or the other causes the torso to twist and bend to the side—this is called **rotation** plus **lateral spinal flexion**. If both sides of the external obliques contract at once, they bend the torso straight forward (spinal flexion).

Internal Obliques

Beneath the external obliques are the *internal obliques,* running at right angles to the fibers above them (Fig. 2-3). If either side of the internal obliques contracts alone, it draws the hip on that side upward toward your centerline. However, the main job of the internal obliques is to help the externals perform twisting motions. In addition, the internals help compress the abdomen, aiding in a variety of internal processes like forced exhalation, coughing, elimination, and childbirth.

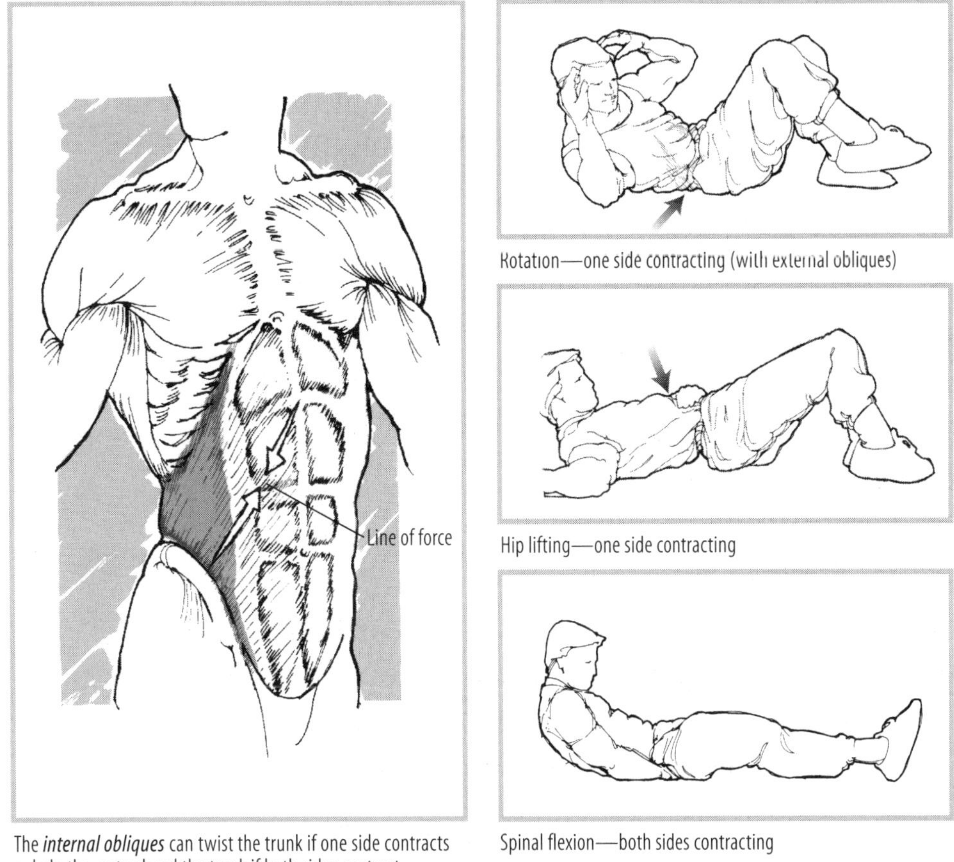

The *internal obliques* can twist the trunk if one side contracts or help the rectus bend the trunk if both sides contract.

Rotation—one side contracting (with external obliques)

Hip lifting—one side contracting

Spinal flexion—both sides contracting

Fig. 2-3 Internal Obliques

Transversalis

The innermost layer of the abs is the *transversalis,* also called the *transversus* muscle. It wraps horizontally around the abdomen from back to front like a girdle, fusing at the centerline (Fig. 2-4). The purpose of the transversalis muscle is to compress the abdomen. Recent studies show it may play an important role in helping to stabilize the spine. However, since there's no way to isolate the transversalis, and since it doesn't contribute to the appearance of abdominal definition, it has little bearing on abdominal training.

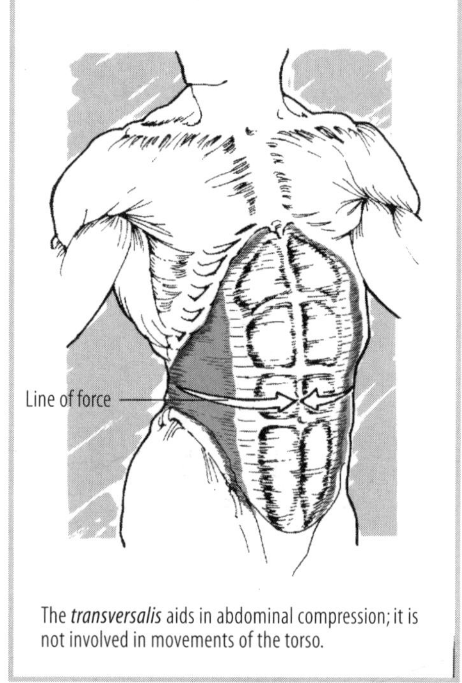

The *transversalis* aids in abdominal compression; it is not involved in movements of the torso.

Fig. 2-4 Transversalis

Together, these four layers of muscle form the **abdominal wall.** The criss-crossing fiber arrangement provides maximum protection against penetration while facilitating an infinite variety of twisting and bending motions of the torso.

SPINAL FLEXION IN DETAIL

The next step is to carefully examine the motions caused by the abs. As mentioned above, their main function is to pull the ribs down and the pelvis up, causing a bend at the waist. This action is called **spinal flexion.** During spinal flexion, the rectus is the main muscle, or **prime mover,** but the internal and external obliques are contracting too.

There are two important points concerning spinal flexion.

First, is the **range of motion** involved. The entire range of flexion that the abs can initiate is only about 30 degrees.

Only 30 degrees... When you lie flat on your back, your upper and lower body form an angle of 180 degrees—in other words, a straight line. By contracting, your abdominals can reduce that to 150 degrees (Fig. 2-5). So, if you're lying on the floor and you fully contract your abs, they will raise your upper torso about a third of the way off the floor—and that's it. *That's all the abs do.*

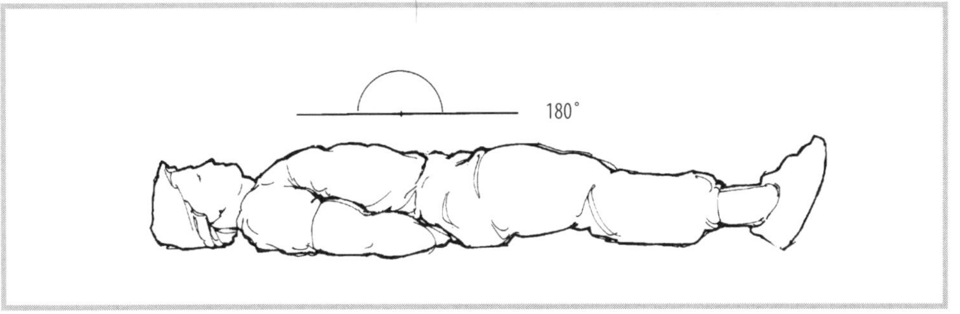

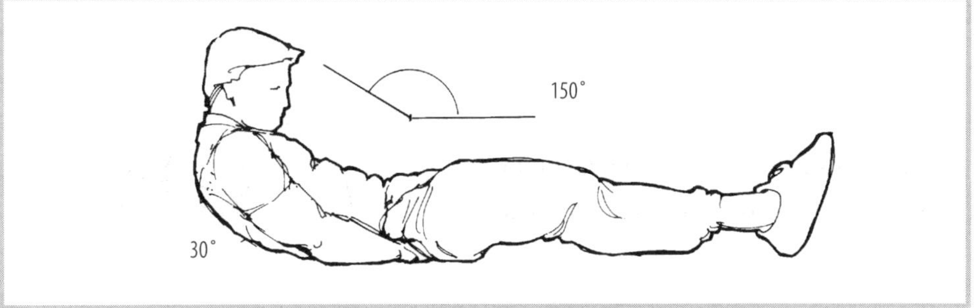

Fig. 2-5 Complete range of motion for the abs is only about 30°

The second important point about the abs' motion is that the "hinge"—in other words, the moving joints—are the lumbar vertebrae of the spine.

These two points are worth driving home once more.

Again, the abs...

- have a range of only 30 degrees
- cause a hinging action in the lower spine

If you're lying down, any raising of the upper body beyond the 30 degree point must involve (1) muscles other than the abs, *and* (2) an additional hinge point at the hip.

In other words, the further you sit up, the less you're using your abs. This explains the inefficiency of many exercises that *appear* to work the abs. Either they involve too wide a range of motion, or they're performed at an angle outside the abs' range.

OLD WAYS DIE HARD

The old-fashioned Straight-Legged Sit-Up, for decades the *only* ab exercise people did, flagrantly violates both these principles. During this exercise, the torso bends nearly 180 degrees—six times the range of the abs—and it hinges, not in the spine, but at the hip joints. As described in Chapter 1, Straight-Legged Sit-Ups mainly work a muscle called the psoas. And because psoas contractions tug at the spine, they can eventually lead to back injury.

Now let's look at another example: the Roman Chair Sit-Up. Like the straight-legged variety, the Roman Chair Sit-Up is an exercise that ignores the mechanical limitations of the abs. In this exercise, the person sits, anchors his or her feet, leans backward slightly, and rocks up and down across a narrow range, hinging at the hips (Fig. 2-6).

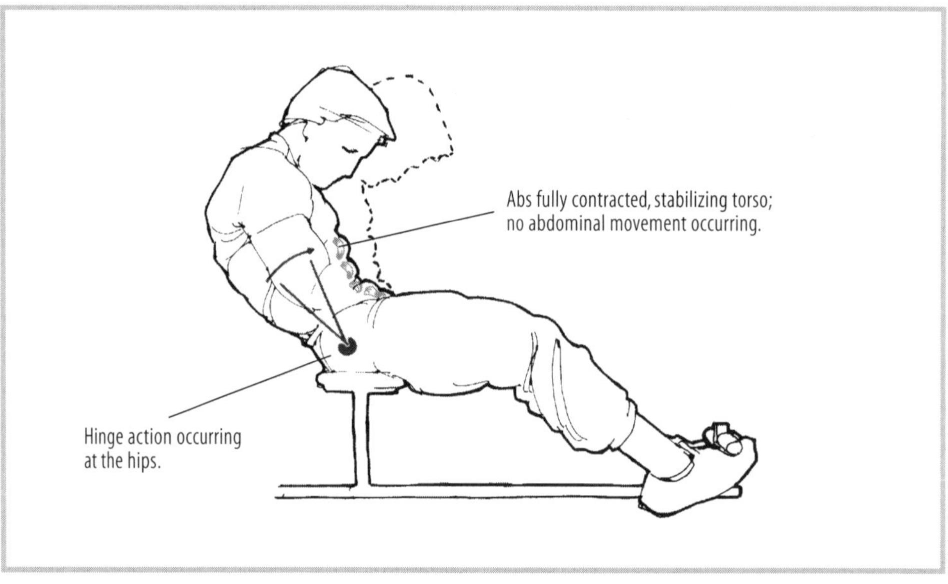

Fig. 2-6 Roman Chair Sit-Ups is mainly a psoas exercise.

This is inefficient in the same way trying to work your forearms by doing biceps curls would be. Sure, forearm muscles are *involved* during a curl, but all they're doing is gripping the bar. The main muscle responsible for the movement—the prime mover—is the biceps. It's the same with Roman Chair Sit-Ups: Although the abdominals do contract, they are acting only as stabilizers and are not responsible for the motion. As an abdominal exercise, *Roman Chair Sit-Ups are 90% wasted effort.*

Summary of Abdominal Anatomy and Function

Muscle:	**Rectus Abdominis**
Location:	Runs from ribs to pubic bone
Function:	Flexes spine

Muscle:	**External Oblique**
Location:	Wraps from back to front, fibers running diagonally downward
Function:	One side contracting bends torso to the side
	One side contracting rotates torso, bringing shoulder of the same side forward
	Both sides contracting flexes spine

Muscle:	**Internal Oblique**
Location:	Wraps from back to front, fibers running diagonally upward
Function:	One side contracting draws hip towards centerline
	One side contracting rotates torso, bringing shoulder of the opposite side forward
	Both sides contracting flexes spine
	Compresses the abdomen

Muscle:	**Transversalis**
Location:	Wraps from back to front, fibers running horizontally
Function:	Compresses the abdomen

Notice again that the abdominals do not attach to the legs. They originate from the ribs, spine, hips, and pubic area, wrapping and crossing the middle body from all angles. The abs cause movements of the upper torso in relation to the pelvis—movements of about 30 degrees or less—and they act as stabilizers during major body motions (more about their stabilizing role in Chapter 5).

Setting Goals: Performance vs. Appearance

Different people have different reasons for training their abs, but most goals come down to **improved athletic performance** or **enhanced appearance**.

From a training standpoint, improved performance requires increased **functional strength**; enhanced appearance calls for improved **tone** and **definition (i.e., fat loss)** with, possibly, some increase in musslce **size**. Your needs will dictate your training strategy.

The basic *Legendary Abs* program focuses on the aesthetic goals. When combined with the *Legendary Abs* High-Low Nutritional Plan and aerobic program in Chapter 4, it will deliver outstanding tone and definition. For those seeking greater sports performance, the Athletic Power Program in Chapters 5 and 6 describes how to train for maximum strength and rotational stability.

FUNCTIONAL STRENGTH

Functional strength refers to the ability to apply strength developed through exercise in daily activity or in the performance of your sport. Functional strength training should aim to increase the strength of the muscles and encourage them to interact in ways that mimic their role as stabilizers in major body movements. Using the basic *Legendary Abs* program, you're bound to increase your functional strength somewhat. But for the ultimate in performance training, see the routines in Chapter 6.

SIZE

When it comes to the aesthetics of the abdominals, most people want good tone and definition without massive gains in size. If this sounds like you, beware of using a progressive overload (ever-increasing amounts of weight). In time, a progressive overload may produce massive, protruding abs, which look like a muscular pot belly. To achieve good tone and definition without excess size takes a high-intensity workout, one *without* ever-increasing resistance. Again, this is how the basic *Legendary Abs* program has been designed.

For some people, of course, size might be a priority. If you are trying to build a generally massive physique, substantial ab development may be necessary for symmetry. You can integrate a gradual weight increase into the routines in the basic *Legendary Abs* program by following the suggestions in the Answers to Frequently-Asked Training Questions in Appendix A.

CUTS

The "cuts" that divide the rectus abdominis into four pairs of lumps are caused by three bands of connective tissue called **tendinous intersections** that cross the face of the muscle. Their exact arrangement is something you're born with. Abdominal exercise will affect the overall size of the lumps, but not their locations or shapes (Fig. 2-7).

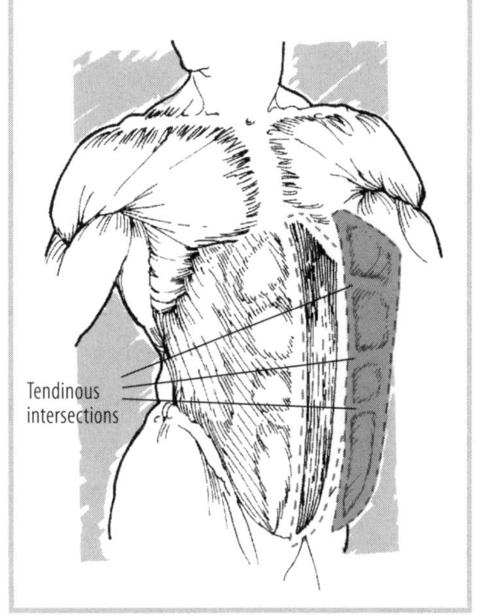

Fig. 2-7 "Cuts" caused by tendinous intersections.

DEFINITION

Definition refers to how sharply cut, chiseled, ripped, or otherwise visible the abs are. How defined you are is a function of how much bodyfat you have.

Everyone has a layer of fat that lies just below the skin and covers his or her abs. The thinner this layer, the better your definition will be. Unfortunately, abdominal exercise will not reduce this fat. People who perform ab exercises without addressing the problem of excess stomach fat may develop toned abs, but the results will remain hidden.

The only effective way to lose excess abdominal fat, or any fat, is with regular aerobic exercise, coupled with sensible eating. A program involving some form of running, walking, swimming, jumping rope, or aerobic dance, along with a moderately low-fat/low-calorie diet is the ideal companion to ab exercise for achieving a lean, well-toned look. (See Chapter 4 for a complete dietary and exercise plan for maximum definition.)

Exercise Mechanics & Performance

Now we're going to delve even deeper into the workings of the abdominals. We'll consider the muscles one by one, exploring their actions and describing the motions best suited to each. Understanding the muscles action will help you perform the exercises more effectively.

RECTUS ABDOMINIS

upper rectus (upper abs)
basic motion: draws rib cage to pelvis

lower rectus (lower abs)
basic motion: draws pelvis to rib cage

Most muscles are attached in such a way that one end is clearly the **fixed end** and the other the **moving end.** The fixed end of the biceps, for instance, is the end that attaches at the shoulder. The biceps' moving end inserts on the forearm. These designations are clear because we almost always see the forearm as moving in relation to the body and not the other way around. When you do a biceps curl, for example, the shoulder (at the fixed end of the muscle) remains stationary while the forearm (at the moving end) is pulled upward (Fig. 2-8).

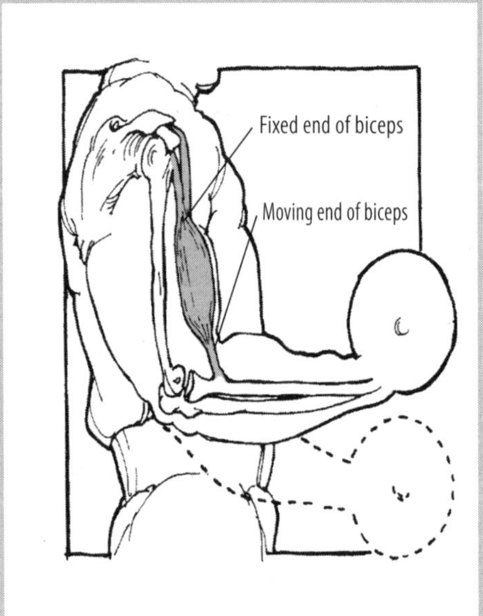

Fig. 2-8

One of the unique features of the abdominal group is that either point of attachment can easily act as the fixed end or the moving end. When the torso moves in relation to a stationary pelvis (as during Crunches), the upper abs are at the moving end. When the pelvis moves in relation to a stationary torso, the lower abs are at the moving end.

Why is this important? In certain muscles, abs among them, growth occurs nearest the moving end. This is because these muscles are stimulated by a different nerve at each end, and the growth happens wherever the stimulation occurs. If you only did Crunches, for instance, most of the resulting abdominal development would occur in your upper abs. This is why it's necessary to do separate upper and *lower* ab exercises.

Four exercises in *Legendary Abs*—Hanging Leg Raises and Knee Raises, Leg Thrusts, and Knee Rock-Backs—are aimed specifically at the lower abs. In all three exercises, the upper body is fixed in position and the lower body (pelvis and legs) is acted on by the moving end of the muscle.

Abdominal Crunches and 1/4 Sit-Ups are the principal *upper* ab motions in the program. In both, the lower body remains fixed while the upper body moves.

The Crunch

Essential in both upper and lower ab work is the Crunch motion (Fig. 2-9), in which pelvis and rib cage are pulled toward each other, and the lower spine tends to round. As mentioned before, part of the reason for the *in*effectiveness of Sit-Ups and many other popular ab exercises is that they involve a *straight* torso, hinging at the hip. In these exercises, the abs do act as stabilizers, but since there's no crunch, they cannot be the prime mover (Fig. 2-10). (Not to mention that all but the first 30 degrees of the Sit-Up exceeds the abs' range of motion!)

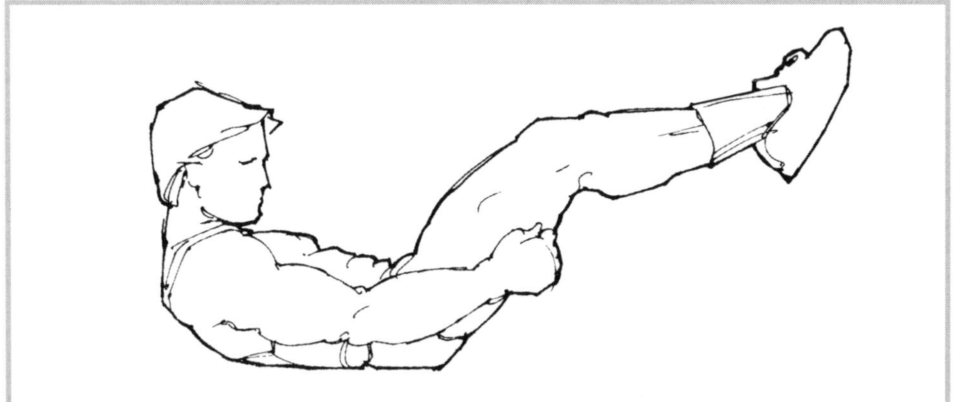

Fig. 2-9 The Crunch

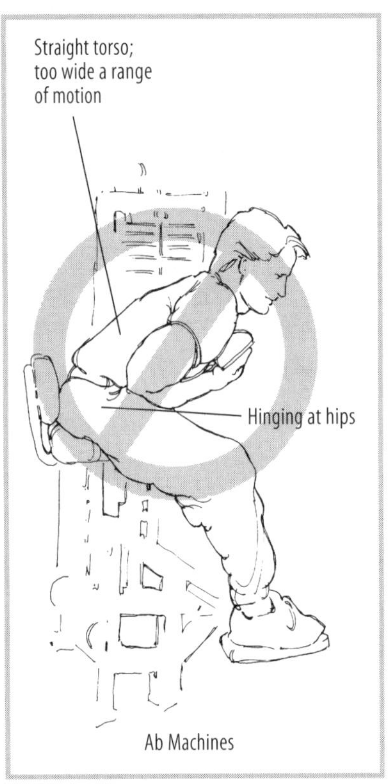

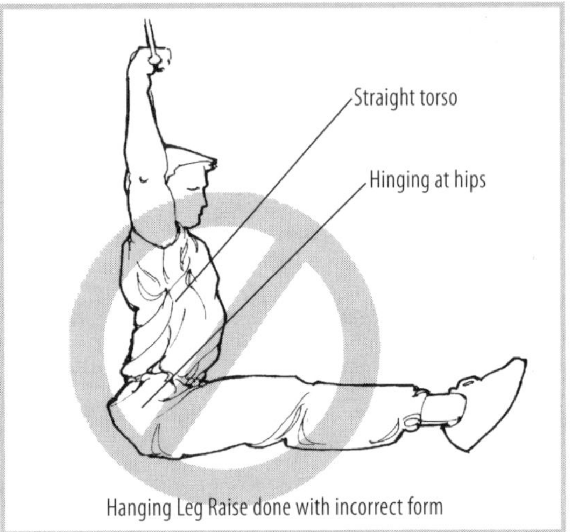

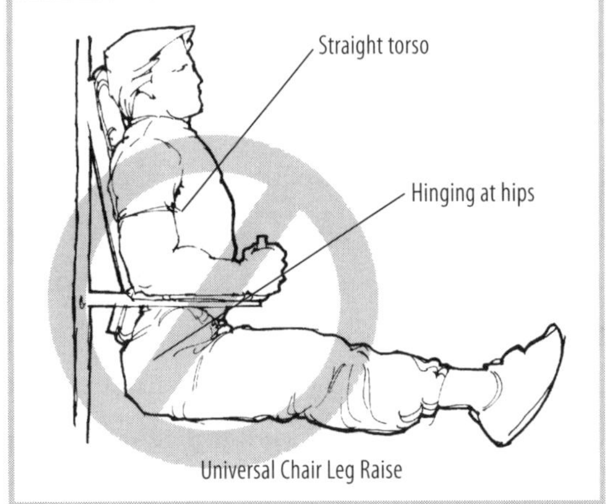

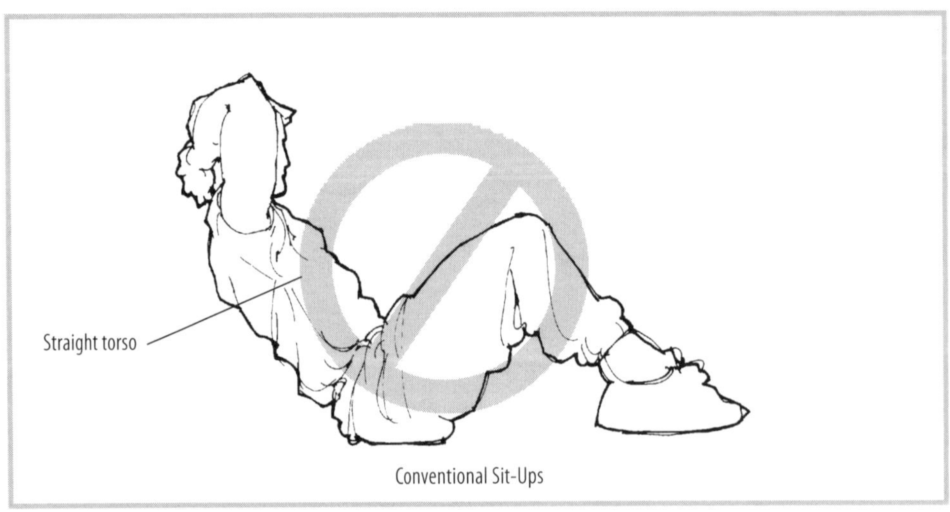

Fig. 2-10 Four inefficient ab exercises

OBLIQUES

external

basic motion: acting together, assists in spinal flexion; each acting alone twists the torso

internal

basic motion: twists the torso; pulls the hip toward the centerline

The obliques mainly act as stabilizers. Certain sports such as wrestling, boxing, and the discus throw require extra-strong obliques and call for a strength-building routine like the one in Chapter 6. In most cases, though, the obliques get a good enough workout just by stabilizing the torso and contributing to trunk flexion during upper and lower ab exercises.

Legendary Abs includes one exercise, Cross-Knee Crunches, that focuses on both internal and external obliques. In combination with the stabilization demands of the other exercises, Cross-Knee Crunches will provide ample oblique development for anyone whose goal is more aesthetic than athletic.

External Oblique Conditioning and Love Handles

Many people make the mistake of trying to "spot reduce" fat bulges from the sides of their waist by doing twisting exercises and side bends. This only makes the bulges worse, by building up muscle beneath the fat layer. *Exercises to avoid:* any involving twisting or bending with weights—because overloading the obliques virtually guarantees a size increase.

If you find yourself developing muscular love handles from too much oblique work, the best thing to do is to stop doing any twisting ab exercise or side bends. The muscles will eventually reduce in size, though slowly.

Remember, reducing excess fat calls for aerobic and dietary measures, not further development of the oblique muscles.

SERRATUS ANTERIOR

The "serrats"—the finger-like muscles on the sides of your rib cage—are not part of the abdominal group. Nevertheless, they are an important part of the look of *Legendary Abs.* They are worked to some extent by the Pull-Down Ab Crunches in the program; however, major pushing motions such as the Bench Press are the best way to increase serratus definition.

Summary

- Growth occurs nearest the moving end of the abs.
- Since either end of the abs can act as the fixed or the moving end, you must do upper *and* lower ab exercises to fully develop your midsection.
- The active ingredient in all ab exercises is the crunch, in which the abs pull the rib cage and pelvis together.
- The stabilization demands placed on the obliques during upper and lower ab exercises, plus Cross-Knee Crunches, are enough to ensure adequate oblique development.
- Overworking the obliques in an attempt to reduce fat will make the problem worse.

Mental Focus During Ab Training

To sustain a high level of intensity during your workout, it's important to approach each exercise with the goal of directing a tightly focused effort at the target muscle. This is only possible if you know, consciously, where the muscle is and how it feels when it contracts. This is **kinesthetic awareness**, a mind-body connection essential to good training.

Visualizing the abdominal layers and their actions is the first step toward developing a keener kinesthetic sense.

ABDOMINALS VS. PSOAS

In particular, your visualization should help you distinguish your abdominals from your psoas, a muscle that attaches to your lower spine (Fig. 2-11) and to your legs, and facilitates jackknife-like movements of the legs and torso. In most daily situations, the abs and psoas work together, but successful ab training should isolate the abs as much as possible.

At first glance, the actions of the psoas and abs appear similar—after all, they both bend the trunk forward. But, in fact, not only are they quite different, they even work against each other to a degree.

We've already seen that when the abs contract, the pelvis and rib cage draw together, resulting in a rounded back (Fig. 2-12). When the psoas muscles contract, they tug on the lower spine and result in an arched back (Fig. 2-13).

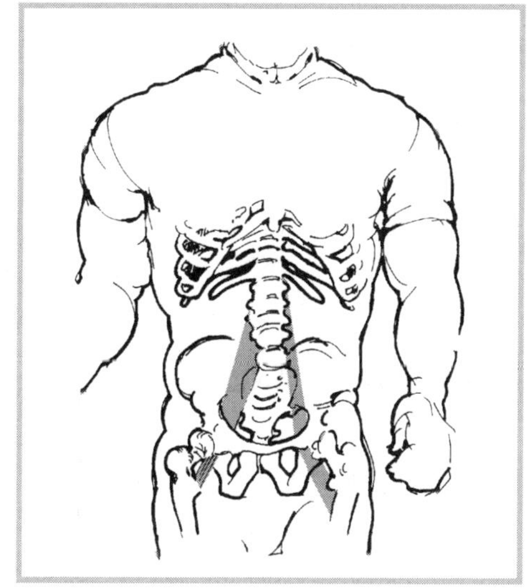

The psoas **Fig. 2-11**

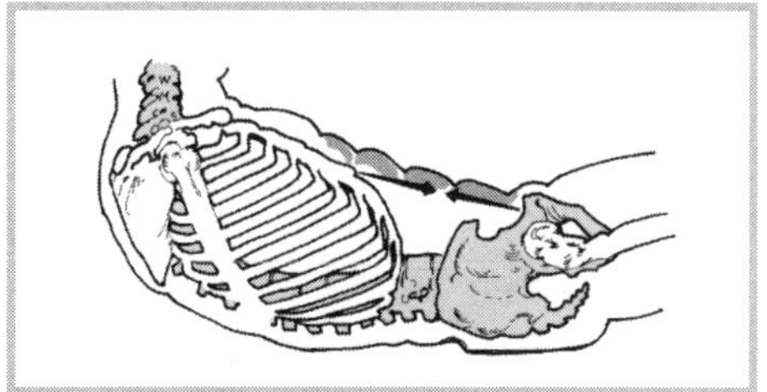

Abs raise torso with hinging action in lower spine

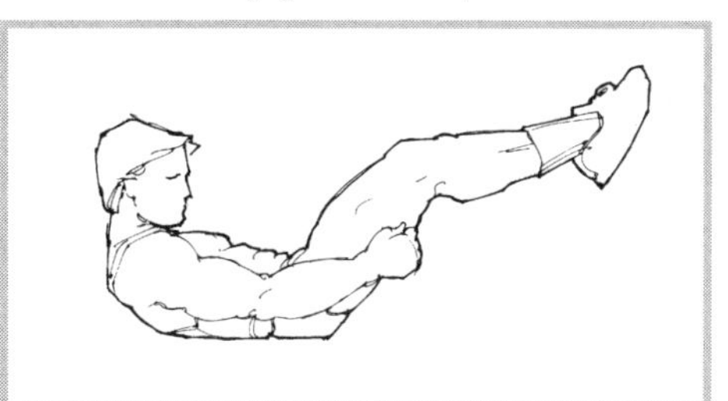

Ab contraction - notice rounded back

Fig. 2-12

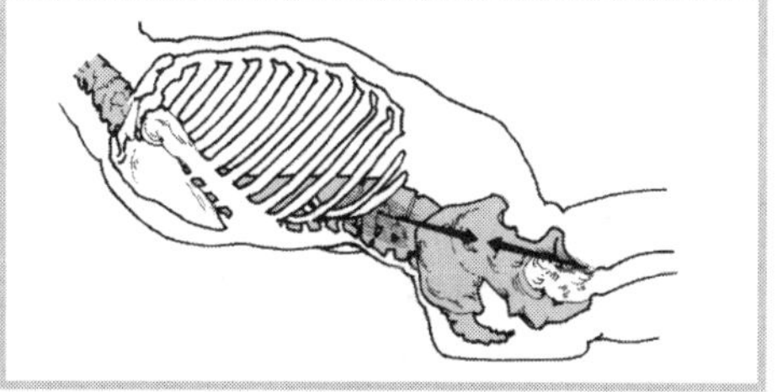

Psoas raise torso with hinging action at hips

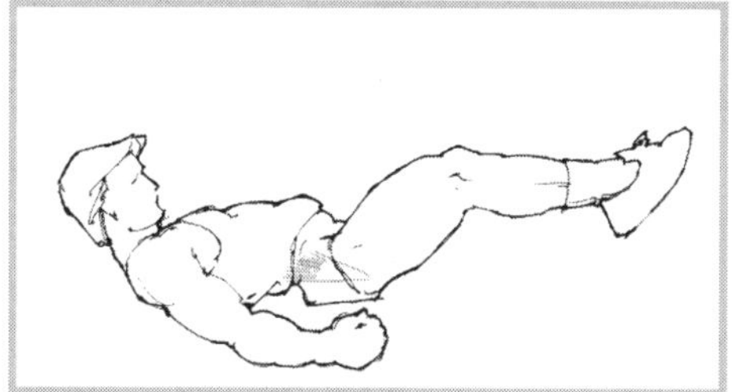

Psoas contraction - notice arched back

Fig. 2-13

These two types of flexion clearly work against each other. Notice how the psoas-dominated Lying Leg Raise in Figure 2-13 effectively stretches the abdominals and makes it almost impossible for them to contract.

But wait! you say. *If the abs don't attach to the legs and the psoas muscles do, it's impossible to do Lying Leg Raises without using the psoas.*

You're right. And this is where the need for accurate mental focus comes in. The abs must *initiate* the motion. After that, the psoas can contribute to it without compromising the abdominal contraction.

Imagine that the goal of Lying Leg Raises is not to raise the legs but to *rock the pelvis upward* with a contraction of the abs. The legs merely follow along. Your legs should always feel as though they are being *supported by the contraction of your abdomen.*

COMMITMENT AND INTENSITY

Apart from the kinesthetic awareness needed to target the abdominals, there is another side to the mental aspect of training, namely, *commitment.* An all-out, fully committed effort causes actual physiological changes that simply walking through the exercises won't.

For instance, one of the main factors limiting a person's training is the accumulation within the muscle cells of waste products—chiefly **lactic acid**, which causes the familiar burn. Of course, it's not possible to keep going indefinitely once lactic acid is being produced and your muscles are screaming with pain. But if you can *tolerate* the burn for a while and regularly push yourself past that point, you will eventually raise the threshold at which your muscle cells begin to form lactic acid and increase the efficiency with which your body gets rid of it.

You can then train with greater intensity, achieving greater results in less time.

Summary

- Abdominal contraction causes the body to hinge in the middle and lower spine, and the back to round.
- Psoas contractions cause the body to hinge at the hip, and the lower back to arch.
- In lower ab exercises that involve the psoas in raising the legs, it's important to focus on the abs to be certain that they, and not the psoas, are initiating the motion.
- High-intensity training causes physiological changes that allow you to achieve greater results in less time.

❖ ❖ ❖

Now that we've covered the basic mechanical system of the abdominals and factors contributing to exercise intensity, it's time to get started! The next chapter will cover the exercises, routines, and schedule.

The Program

This chapter presents the actual *Legendary Abs* program—the exercises, routines, and schedule needed to build great abdominal tone and definition in less than 6 minutes a workout—even at the highest levels!

You may already be familiar with some of the exercises described here. But the exercises alone are not what make *Legendary Abs* so effective. The real power comes from the way the exercises are combined in the routines. It is the sequence, timing, and overall progression that make this program so powerful. Even if you've done some of these exercises before, you'll be amazed at how much more effective they become when done exactly as indicated in the *Legendary Abs* routines.

3

THE PROGRAM

Hanging Leg Raises

Main muscle trained: lower region of rectus abdominis ("lower abs")

For this exercise, you'll need a horizontal bar from which to hang. A doorway chinning bar will work, but a higher bar is better. Ideally, your legs should be able to hang straight without touching the ground. *(For suggestions on what to do if you don't have a hanging bar, see Appendix A.)*

STARTING POSITION

Grip the bar with hands slightly wider than shoulder width apart, and hang.

THE MOVEMENT

With knees slightly bent, raise your legs as high as you can (Fig. 3-1a). Note: The raising of the legs starts with a curling movement of the pelvis, which should remain tilted forward throughout the exercise. This forward movement of the pelvis is crucial—without it, the psoas muscles, not the abs, are doing most of the work (Fig 3-1b).

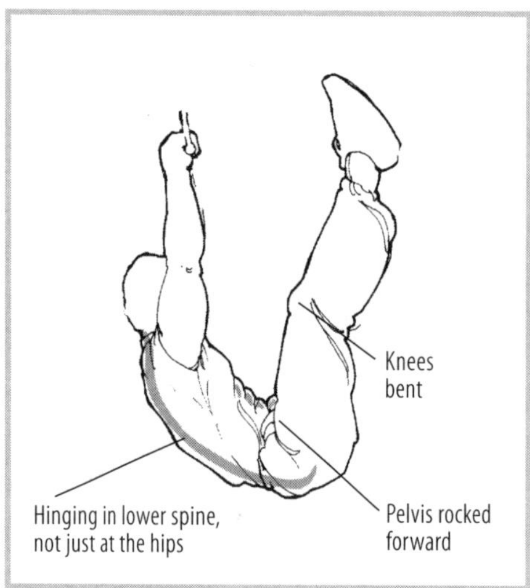

Fig. 3-1a Hanging Leg Raises—correct

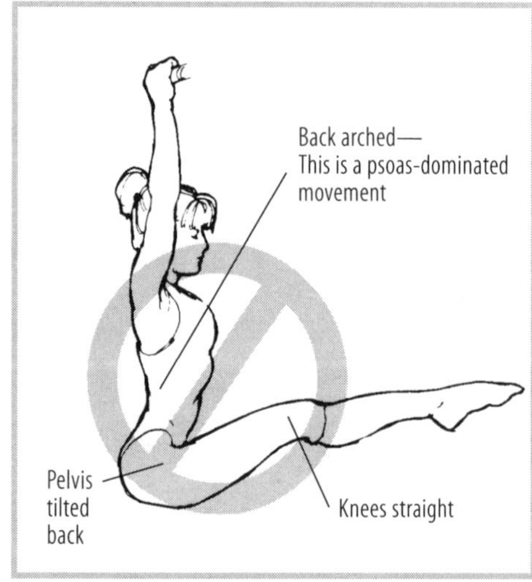

Fig. 3-1b Wrong

Hold for one second at the peak, and lower. Be sure to keep your pelvis tilted forward on the way down also. When you reach the bottom of the rep, your back should still be rounded.

Perform the reps slowly enough that your body doesn't swing. Also, keep your upper torso as relaxed as possible: resist the temptation to do a partial pull-up with each rep, as this wastes energy and shifts your focus off the abs.

To make it easier:

At first, it's all right to use a slight swinging motion as an assist (Fig. 3-1c,d). This will relieve stress on the lower back and will help you force out enough reps to begin to build lower ab strength without sacrificing form. Use as little swing as you can (ideally, no more than 6–12 inches). **Important:** Don't let your back arch when you swing. Your pelvis should remain tucked slightly forward at all times. When you raise your legs, imagine it's your *pelvis* you're trying to raise first and that your legs are just along for the ride.

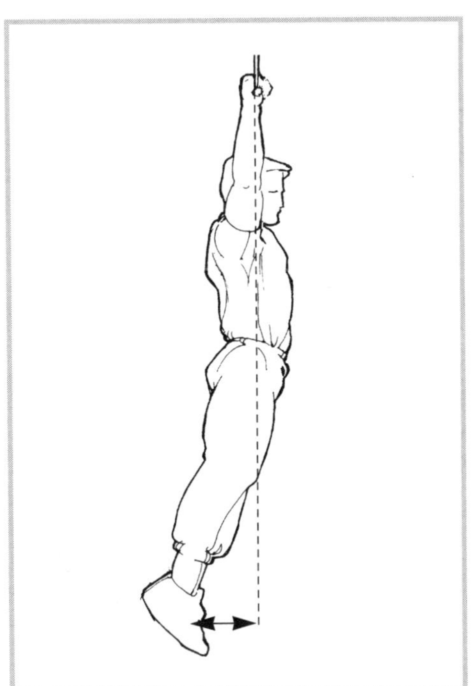

Body swings back as a unit, 6–12 inches

Legs should separate at the bottom of the movement

Fig. 3-1c,d Using swinging as an assist

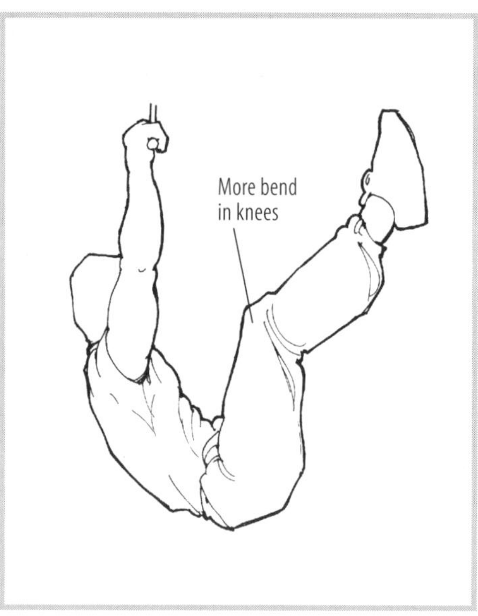

Fig. 3-1e

You can also make the motion a little easier at first by increasing the bend in the knees (Fig.3-1e).

To make it harder:

- Use no swing at all.
- Maintain only a slight bend in your knees.
- Make the descending movement slower than the ascending movement.

Hanging Knee-Ups

Main muscle trained: lower region of rectus abdominis ("lower abs")

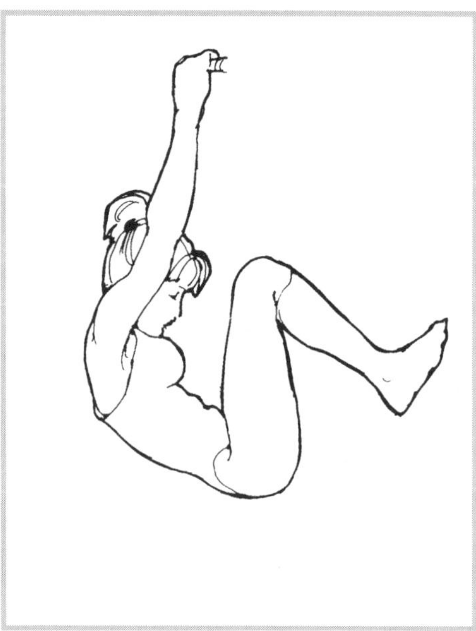

Fig. 3-2

Hanging Knee-Ups are identical to Hanging Leg Raises, except that here you fully bend you knees as you lift, and, if you can, lift them all the way to your chest (Fig. 3-2). The purpose is to get the maximum range of abdominal contraction by curling your pelvis as much as possible.

EQUIPMENT NOTE: Devices to reduce arm strain

If you find that your arm, hand, or shoulder strength limit your ability to hang, consider one of the following training aids:

Wrist Straps

Wrist straps, or weight-lifting straps, come in a variety of designs. The simplest are canvas strips that wrap around the wrist and around the bar (Fig. 3-3). They take much of the stress off the forearm muscles—the "gripping muscles" of the hand.

To use, wrap the straps several times around the bar and grip them. You should only need to grip the straps tightly enough to keep them from unravelling. If the straps are positioned correctly, you should feel the stress transferred to your wrists.

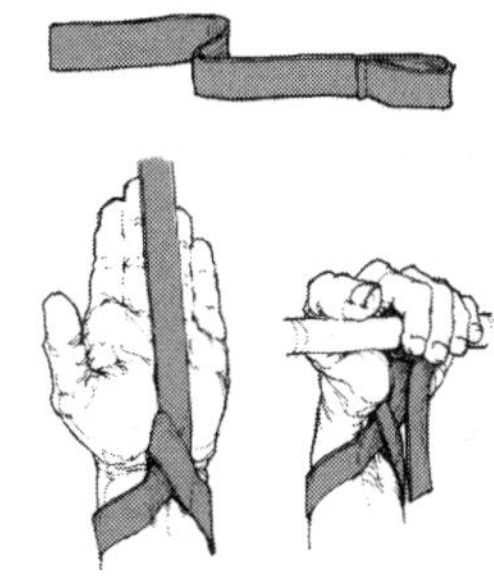

Wrap strap around bar and grip it. Strap takes weight, rather than forearm muscles.

Fig. 3-3 Weight Training Straps

Arm Slings

Arm slings, or arm straps, are loops of leather or fabric that hang from a chinning bar (Fig. 3-4). They're a good way to spare your arms the stress of hanging, but they must be used carefully because they can encourage your back to arch, increasing psoas involvement. If you use arm slings, make a special effort to maintain an upward tilt of your pelvis to prevent your back from arching.

To use, slide your arms through the loops to a point just below your armpits; you may need to stand on a stool to do this. The farther in you can comfortably place the straps, the less effort it will take to hold yourself in position. Wearing a sweatshirt helps protect your skin from possible abrasion.

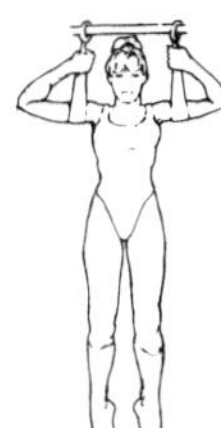

WRONG! Too much psoas

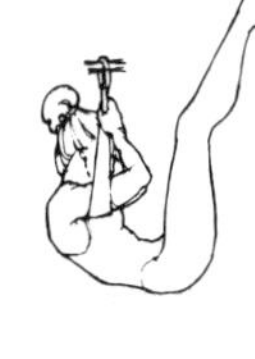

Correct

Fig. 3-4 Arm Slings

HFL Lying Leg Thrusts

Main muscle trained: lower region of rectus abdominis ("lower abs")

This exercise is our variation of the traditional Lying Leg Raise. We believe it offers several advantages:

- It has a wider range of motion, making it easier to fully involve the abs.
- It is more versatile, offering more ways to modify it to make it easier or harder.
- It uses momentum, which helps to build explosive power in the target muscles.
- It significantly reduces stress on the lower back.

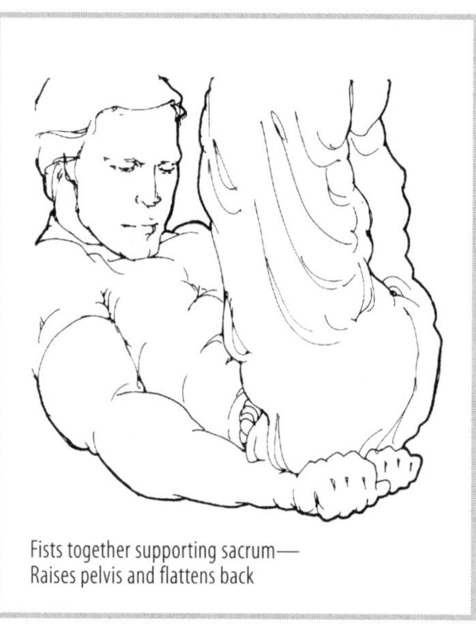

Fists together supporting sacrum—
Raises pelvis and flattens back

Fig. 3-5a The cradle

Lie on your back on a soft mat or carpet. While getting in position, keep your knees bent and your fleet flat on the floor. Place your fists under your pelvis on either side of your tailbone, palms down. Your fists should form a cradle that serves to tip your pelvis up toward your stomach and flatten your lower spine to the floor (Fig. 3-5a).

Once your hips are elevated by the cradle, raise your head—and shoulders, if possible—slightly off the ground. This requires abdominal strength and will make the exercise harder. It will also make it virtually impossible for your back to arch, thereby guaranteeing maximum ab involvement.

If you're not quite strong enough yet to raise your head and shoulders, start gradually. Raise only your head and do fewer reps. Five reps with good form are better than fifty without. Eventually, the strength will come.

STARTING POSITION

Raise your legs about 14 to 18 inches off the floor—high enough that you can feel your lower back flatten. Bend your knees slightly. If you feel any tendency to arch your back, start higher and/or increase the bend in your knees (Fig. 3-5b).

THE MOVEMENT

Raise your legs by curling your pelvis up toward your ribs, until your feet point straight up (Fig. 3-5b). Don't let your feet travel past the vertical point.

At this point, thrust upward from your pelvis, as though trying to stamp your footprints on the ceiling (Fig. 3-5c). Then, drop straight down, retracing the path, and allow your legs to return to the starting position (Fig. 3-5d).

Each rep should feel like a two-part action: an upswing and a vertical thrust. Keep the parts distinct: swing, thrust—then, coming down: drop pelvis, drop legs.

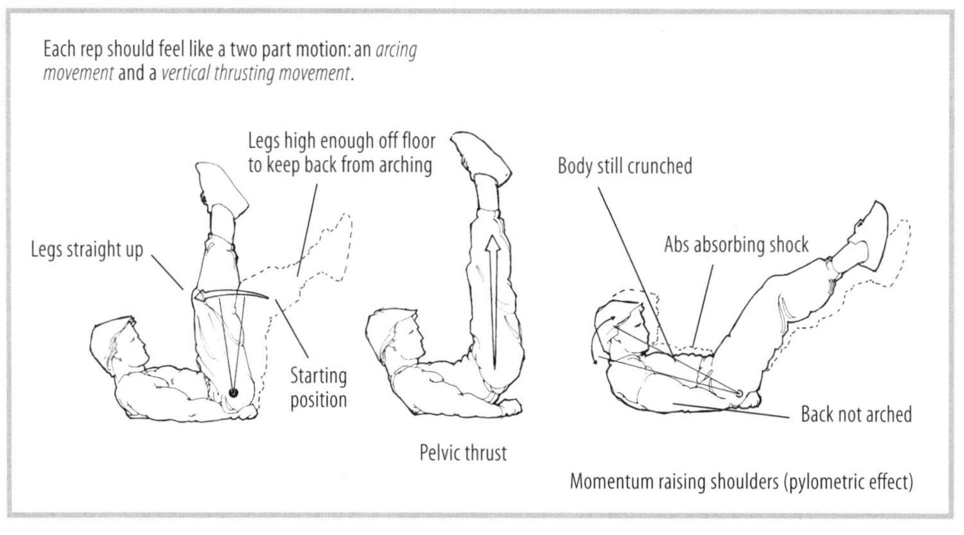

Fig. 3-5b **Fig. 3-5c** **Fig. 3-5d**

To make it easier:

Start with your legs high (two to three feet from the ground) and accelerate on the way up, using the momentum to make the final thrust. Continue through the peak of the rep without a pause. As you drop your legs, keep their speed under control—put the brakes on slightly—so the change of direction at the bottom is not too abrupt.

EQUIPMENT NOTE: The Legendary Abs Crunchbelt

Because of the tendency of the lower back to arch during HFL Leg Thrusts, we recommend using your fists to form a "cradle" beneath your tailbone. This lifts the pelvis and forces the lower back to remain flat on the floor.

The Crunchbelt (Fig. 3-6a) provides a firm, springy cushion to take the place of your fists. When used correctly, the Crunchbelt is more effective and more comfortable than using your hands for support. Plus, it can be used during crunches, when your hands are normally positioned behind your head.

To use, place the pad behind your back with the point of the "V" at the very tip of your spine. The upper arms of the "V" should rest just below the two bony protruberences on either side of your spine, just below your waist. Bring the straps around your hips (not your waist), and adjust them to buckle snugly in front. **Note:** The Crunchbelt should *not* rest in the small of your back.

Fig. 3-6a

Perform Lying Leg Thrusts as described on page 45. As you descend from the peak of each rep, the Crunchbelt should provide support and also give you a little bounce at the bottom of the rep (Fig. 3-6b). Be sure not to drop your legs with such force that your back arches. Remember, your back should remain flat and your pelvis elevated at all times; there should be no see-saw motion over the pad. If you discover that your pelvis is rolling over the pad at the bottom of the rep, stop immediately and reposition the pad lower on your hips.

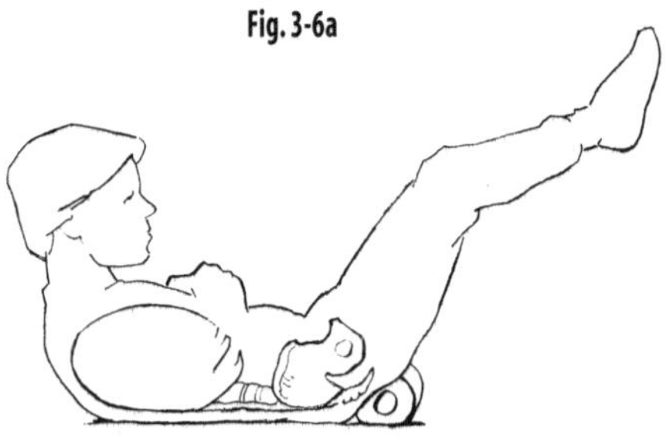

Fig. 3-6b

To make it harder:

Use rhythm: The up motion should decelerate as it nears the top; it should hold for a second at the peak and accelerate on the way down. The change of direction at the bottom should be sudden. Concentrate on fully absorbing the momentum at the bottom of the rep with your abs, not with your back. Try to achieve a slight rocking motion of the entire body so that as your legs drop, your head and shoulders rise—in a one-piece, see-saw motion, with your center body maintaining enough contraction that your back never arches (Fig. 3-5d).

Abdominal Crunches

Main muscle trained: upper region of rectus abdominis ("upper abs")

Lie in standard bent-knee sit-up position (Fig. 3-7a) and very slowly raise your shoulders and upper back about 30 degrees off the ground (Fig. 3-7b). Your upper body should curl forward as though you are trying to touch your chin to your navel. Hold for about one second. Return to starting position.

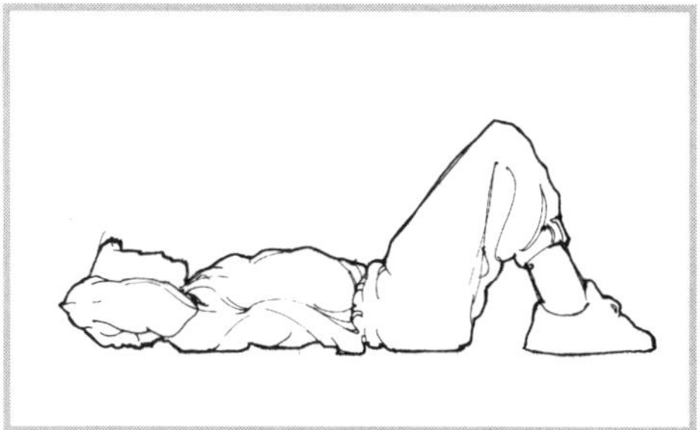

Fig. 3-7a

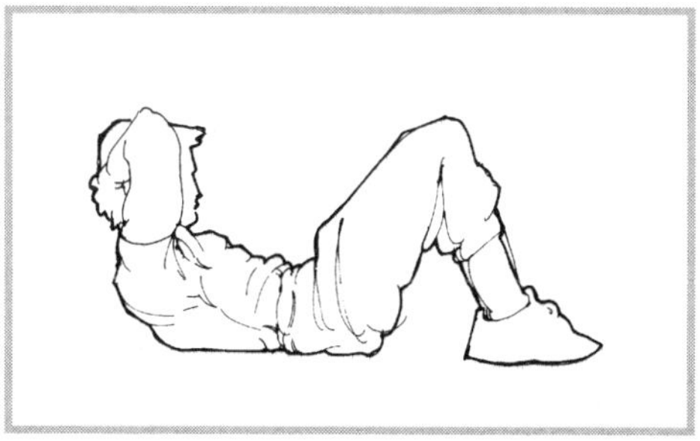

Fig. 3-7b

Throughout the motion, keep your arms in place (palms against the back of your head, elbows out) but as relaxed as possible. Do not pull against the back of your head. Pulling won't make the movement any easier—it will simply put unnecessary stress on your neck. Holding your hands suspended on either side of your head is a good way to avoid pulling on your head. Also, don't try to flap your elbows or shoot your head forward to generate momentum.

Note: *Raising your shoulders* means actually lifting your shoulder blades, not just rounding your shoulders forward as you lift your neck (Fig. 3-7c). Until some part of the torso leave the ground, you're not exercising your abs!

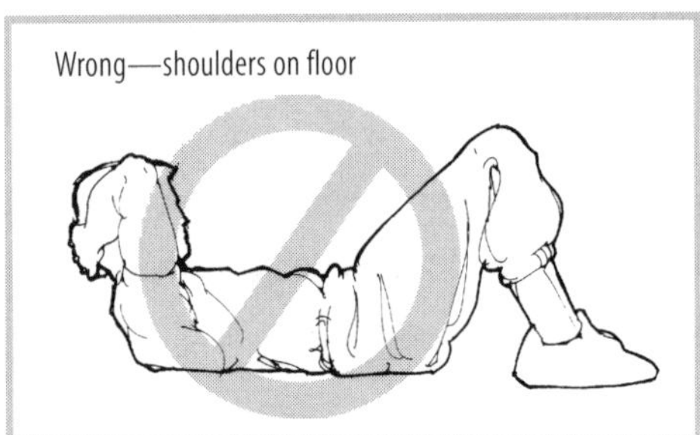

Fig. 3-7c

Working at a moderately slow pace will ensure the exercise's intensity. One full rep should take at least 2 seconds.

To make it easier:

Notice that Crunches and 1/4 Sit-Ups (page 51), though similar, each have a slightly different focus. Crunches, as described above, involve an upward curling motion of the torso. In 1/4 Sit-Ups, however, the head, neck, and shoulders are raised vertically, as though a string were attached to your breastbone, pulling you straight up. To make your routine a little easier, reverse the focus of these two exercises: Do Crunches with a vertical lift (Fig 3-7d) and 1/4 Sit-Ups with an upward curl.

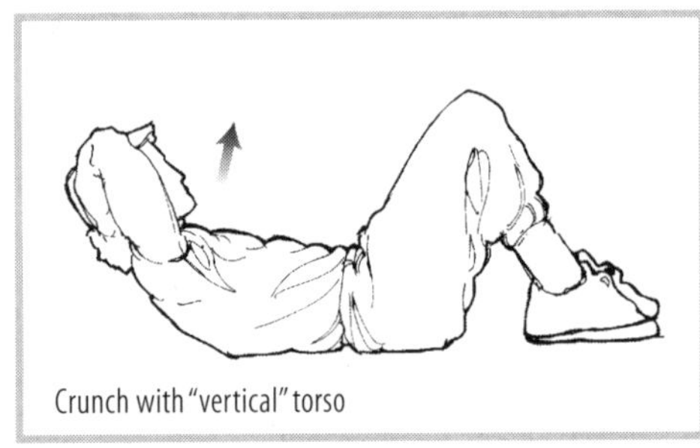

Fig. 3-7d

Another way to make crunches easier is plant your feet a little further away from your body, there by increasing your ballast length.

To make it harder:

By bringing your feet closer in to your body, you decrease your ballast length and make the exercise harder. In addition, a 5- or 10-pound plate may be held behind the head to increase the overload. However, don't increase the weight unless you want to build abdominal *size* as well as definition.

Cross-Knee Abdominal Crunches

Main muscle trained: external and internal obliques

Lie in bent-knee sit-up position (Fig 3-8a) and slowly raise your shoulders, upper back, and *right hip*. Twist your torso so your right shoulder aims toward your left knee (Fig. 3-8b). Feel for a contraction along the right side of the abdomen. Hold for at least a second; then slowly return to the starting position. Alternate sides.

Fig. 3-8a

Fig. 3-8b

There are really two aspects of this motion that function together to work both internal and external obliques. To help you perfect your form and get the most out of the exercise, these are described separately below. **Note:** This exercise works best if the hands are not clasped behind the head but simply raised on either side of the head. This allows the upper body to be more flexible.

ASPECT #1 TORSO ROTATION

Main muscle activated: external obliques (plus some internal)

As you lift your head and shoulders from the floor, twist your chest about 45 degrees to one side. If you're turning to the right, you should feel the contraction occurring to the left of the centerline. Try placing the palm of your hand over this area and adjust the angle of your body until you feel the maximum contraction in the external oblique (Fig. 3-8c). The more twist you can achieve, the more pronounced the contraction will be.

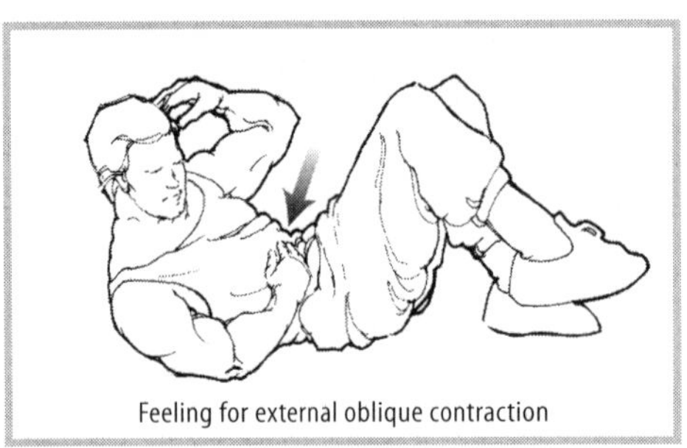

Feeling for external oblique contraction

Fig. 3-8c

To help yourself get a better sense of the external oblique's action, use your palm to feel the difference between *twisting* the torso and *raising it straight up* (which uses mostly the rectus abdominis). Work at both of these until you feel a difference, and try to make that difference as big as possible.

ASPECT #2 HIP ELEVATION

Main muscle activated: internal obliques (plus some external)

To experience the *internal* oblique contribution to this exercise, lie in the starting position again and press lightly with your fingers just above the pelvic bone on both sides of your waist. Raise your right hip off the floor. You should feel a distinct contraction in the muscle on that side (Fig. 3-8d). Since contracting the gluteus muscles will also cause the hip to lift, make sure your buttocks are relaxed. One way to help isolate the internal oblique is to lift your left foot an inch or two from the floor at the same time you lift your right hip.

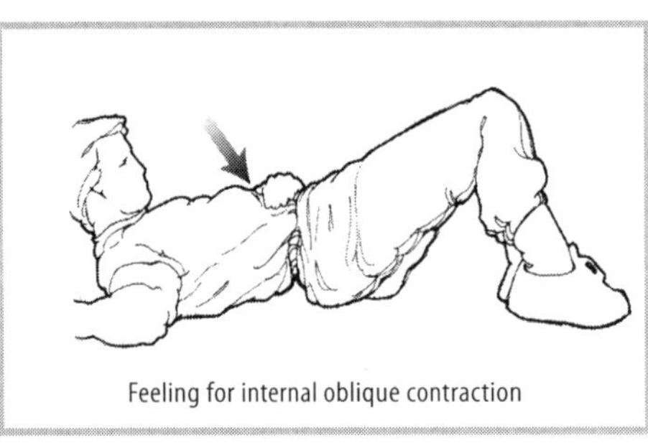

Feeling for internal oblique contraction

Fig. 3-8d

Using these techniques to develop a kinesthetic sense of the difference between the internal and external obliques will help you to get maximum benefit from the exercise.

To make it harder:

Slightly lift the foot on the side of the body on which the internal oblique is contracting. In other words, when you twist to the left, raise your left foot (in addition to your right hip), and vice versa (Fig 3-8e). This may sound confusing, but a little practice will make it clear!

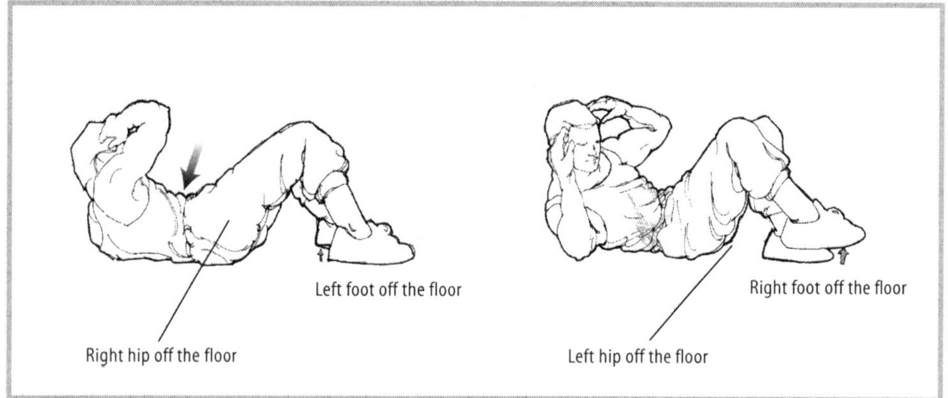

Fig. 3-8e Making it harder—raising foot off the floor

1/4 Sit-Ups

Main muscle trained: upper region of the rectus abdominis ("upper abs")

Lie on your back with legs elevated so that your hips and your knees both form right angles (Fig 3-9a). Raise and lower your torso as quickly as you can. **Note:** Don't let your legs drift—too much variation in the angle of the legs (Fig. 3-9b,c) can drastically reduce the effectiveness of this exercise!

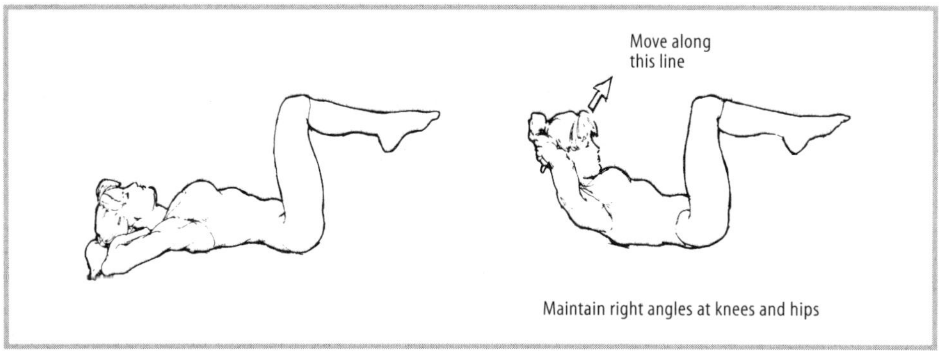

Fig. 3-9a

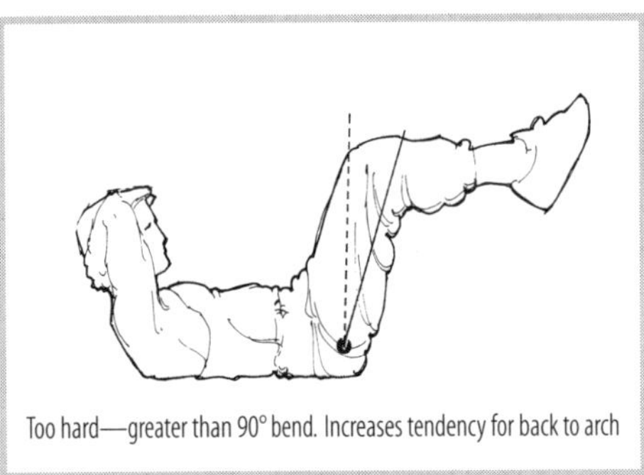

Too hard—greater than 90° bend. Increases tendency for back to arch

Fig. 3-9b

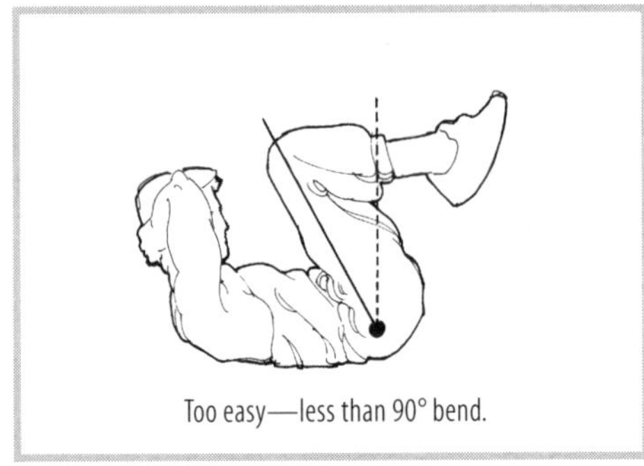

Too easy—less than 90° bend.

Fig. 3-9c

An important difference between these and Abdominal Crunches is that in this case you should think "up" with the torso, rather than "to the knees," as you do during Crunches. This varies the stress on the abs and assures greater definition.

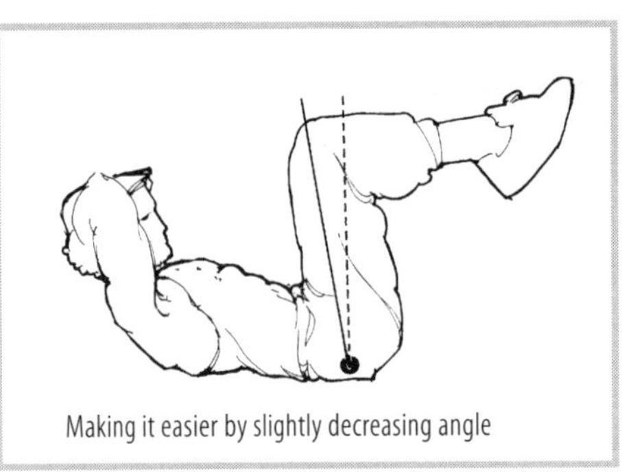

Making it easier by slightly decreasing angle

Fig. 3-9d

To make it easier or harder:

Although the angle of your legs should ideally remain at 90 degrees, it may be deliberately varied within a narrow range (not more than 1 or 2 inches), according to your needs. Pulling the knees slightly closer in will make the exercise easier (Fig. 3-9d); pushing them slightly farther out will make it harder.

Knee Rock-Backs

Main muscle trained: upper and lower rectus abdominis

The purpose of Knee Rock-Backs is to finish off both upper and lower abs at the end of the routine. It is a *plyometric* motion—involving sudden changes of direction—and spans the entire range of the muscle. This exercise helps increase the intensity at the more advanced levels of the course.

STARTING POSITION

The starting position is similar to that of Lying Leg Thrusts, except that your knees should point straight up and your feet should be about 12 inches from the floor (Fig. 3-10a). As you did with Leg Thrusts, form a cradle with your hands to support your pelvis and keep your back from arching at the bottom of the movement, or use the *Legendary Abs* Crunchbelt.

THE MOVEMENT

Rock your feet up over your head. At the peak of the motion, only your shoulders (and arms) will be touching the ground (Fig. 3-10b). Rock back down. When your feet reach their starting level, forcefully reverse the direction and begin another rep.

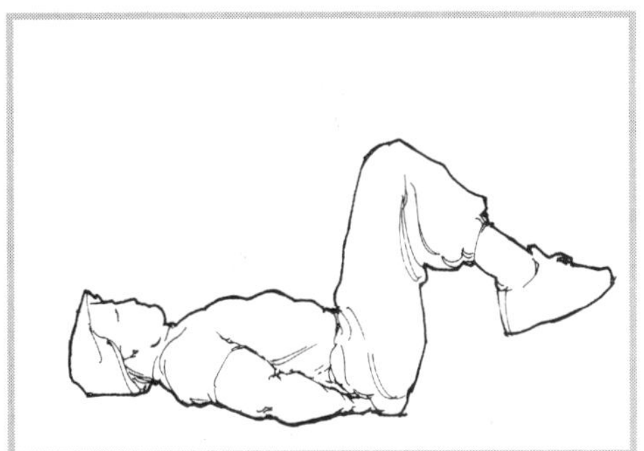

Fig. 3-10a

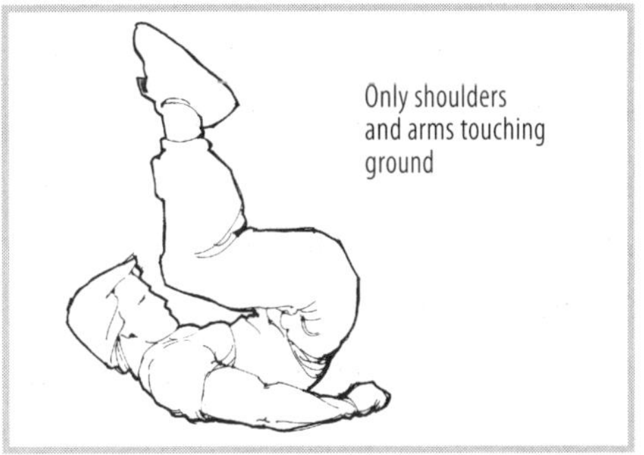

Fig. 3-10b

Several points to observe:

- Make the change of direction at the bottom of each rep abrupt. It should feel like a bounce. As during Leg Thrusts, however, your back should not arch.
- Try not to push against the ground with your arms at the top of the rep; the force of the movement should come from your abs. Concentrate on feeling an abdominal crunch.
- As you rock, visualize the crunch traveling up and down like a wave along the length of the rectus abdominis.

Pull-Down Ab Crunches

Main muscles trained: upper region of the rectus abdominis, assisted by serratus anterior.

This last exercise is optional. Requiring equipment found in most gyms, it is included for bodybuilders or those who wish to fine-tune their abs.

It can be done:

- using a constant load, to add to the intensity of your training program and help build greater definition; or
- using a gradually increasing load, as part of an effort to gain size.

Attach a double-handled rope to an overhead pulley, or drape a towel over a lat bar so that by grasping both ends you can pull the bar down (Fig 3-11a). To fully involve the serratus anterior (the finger-like muscles on the sides of your ribcage), your forearms should be as close together as possible.

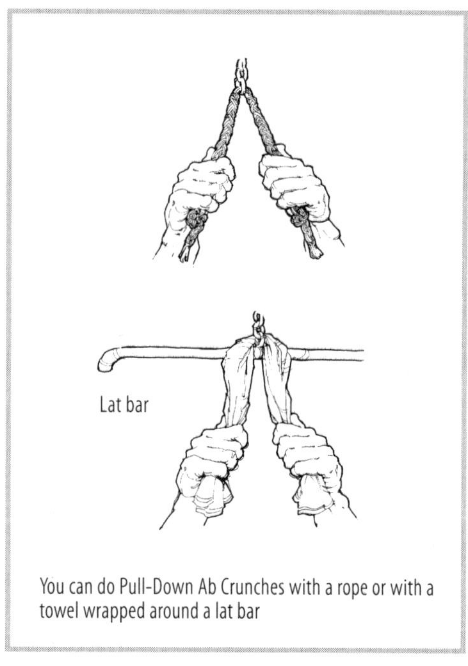

You can do Pull-Down Ab Crunches with a rope or with a towel wrapped around a lat bar

Fig. 3-11a

STARTING POSITION

Kneel about 18 inches out from the spot directly below the pulley (Fig. 3-11b). The cable should travel at a slight angle away from the machine to your hands.

THE MOVEMENT

Keeping your hands against the top of your head, hunch over until your elbows come about a quarter of the way to your knees (Fig. 3-11c). Remember, the abs only have a 30-degree range of motion, so don't pull the rope to the floor, as you sometimes see people do (Fig. 3-11d). Pull down as though you are trying to hunch your shoulders and chest over a bar held at chest level. This will maximize ab involvement and minimize the psoas' contribution.

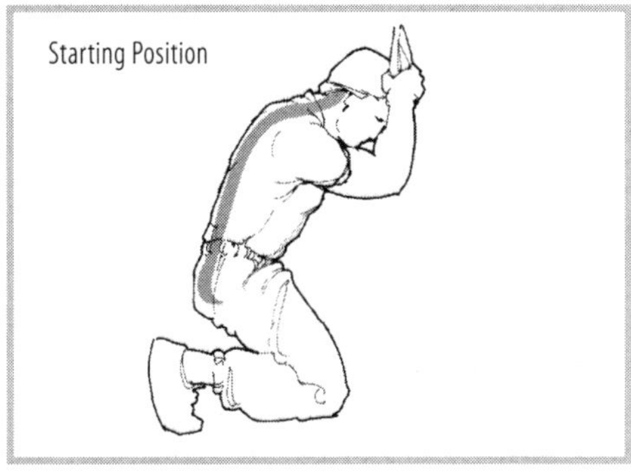

Fig. 3-11b

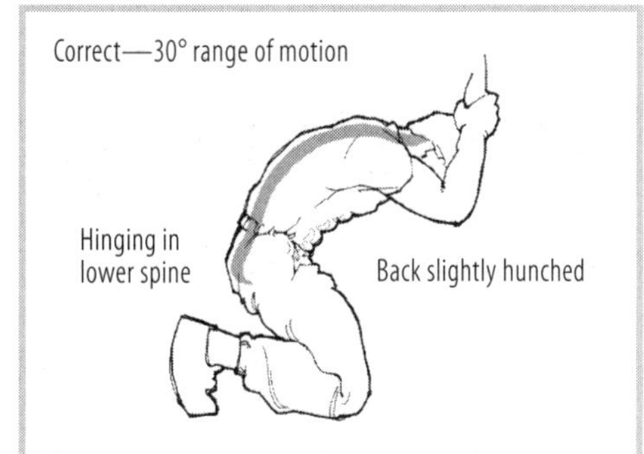

Fig. 3-11c

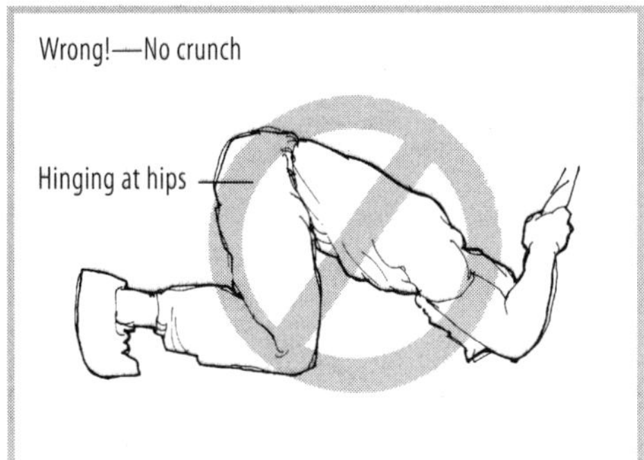

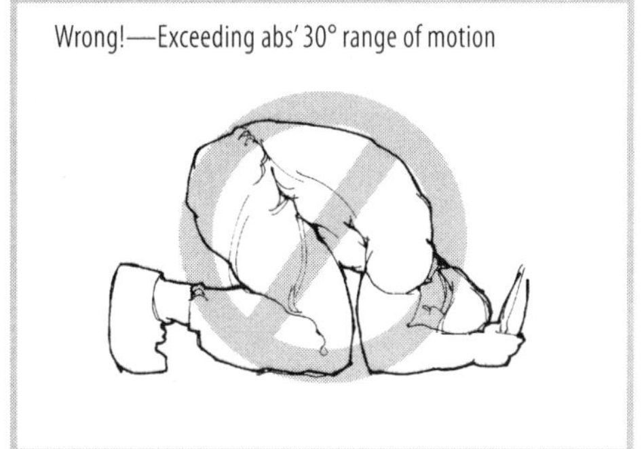

Fig. 3-11d

EQUIPMENT NOTE: Elastic Straps

Pull-Down Ab Crunches can also be done using an elastic band to provide resistance. Drape the band over the top of your chinning bar, a low tree branch, etc., grip both ends (Fig. 3-12), and do the exercise as described. **Always use caution and protect your face when training with an elastic strap!**

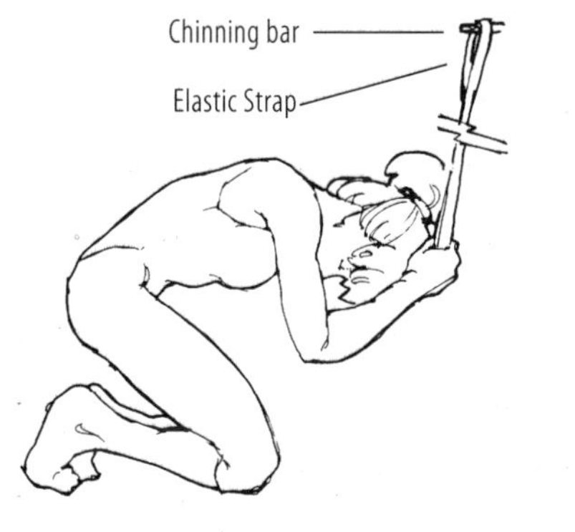

Fig. 3-12

Remember what Abdominal Crunches (Fig. 3-7) felt like? Try to achieve the same motion here—the same crunch in the upper abs.

Hyperextensions

Main muscle trained: spinal erectors

Throughout the body, muscle groups work in pairs to maintain a balance of strength around joints. The spinal erector muscles act to straighten your back, pulling in opposition to your abs. A proper balance of strength between abs and spinal erectors will ensure good posture and a balanced distribution of stress in daily activity.

Hyperextensions are best done on a special bench (found in most gyms). With a little ingenuity, it's also possible to do them on the edge of a resilient surface like a padded table, with someone holding your ankles.

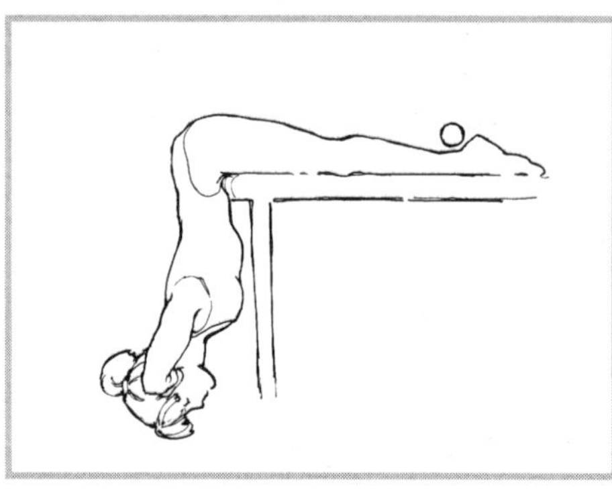

Fig. 3-13a

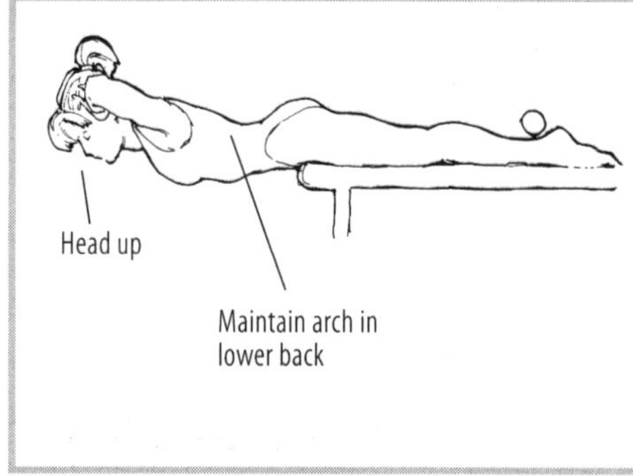

Fig. 3-13b

Lie face down, bent at the waist, hanging over the edge of the bench (Fig. 3-13a). Lightly rest your hands behind your head or neck, and slowly straighten your body to a horizontal position (Fig. 3-13b). Don't come up any higher than this.

Throughout the motion, keep your head and shoulders arched backward, as in a swan dive. Don't try to lace your fingers together behind your neck; this makes it impossible to fully arch the upper back. If you maintain the proper arch, your fingers will probably just barely reach the sides of your head.

THE ROUTINES

If you are just starting to train for the first time, start at Level A. If you've worked your abs before, but your previous training has not included *correctly executed* Hanging Leg Raises (see page 40 for correct form), start at Level 1. To get the benefit of the higher levels of the program, it's essential to perform Hanging Leg Raises correctly. Don't shortchange yourself! Even if you're an experienced trainer, you'll get better results if you build from the ground up.

WHEN TO MOVE UP

Try to get as much out of each level as possible. There's no advantage to jumping up levels before you need to—you'll just be working harder for the same results. Although it's necessary to overload the muscles to get results, overloading too much too fast just wastes energy and increases the risk of injury.

Move to a new level when the one you're on becomes easy and you're no longer getting results. Unless both of these conditions exist, stay where you are. To help you decide when it's time to move up, take the appropriate self evaluation test in Appendix B.

SPEED KEYS AND RESTS

The relative speeds of exercises in these routines have been carefully balanced to maximize the effectiveness of the program. For best results, perform each exercise at the speed listed. (f) = fast (about 2 reps per second) / (m) = medium (about 1 rep per second) / (s) = slow (about 1 rep per 2 seconds).

In practice, a fast pace for one exercise may be different from a fast pace for another. Treat these rep/sec guidelines as averages; don't feel you need to match them exactly. Another way to look at it: *Fast* means as fast as you can do a particular exercise. *Medium* means about half that speed. *Slow* means about one-quarter that speed.

Except where indicated, routines should be done with no rest between exercises.

Level A

1 Set	**HFL Lying Leg Thrusts**	15 reps (m)	
1 Set	**1/4 Sit-Ups**	25 reps (s)	*10 sec. rest*
1 Set	**HFL Lying Leg Thrusts**	10 reps (m)	
1 Set	**1/4 Sit-Ups**	20 reps (m)	

Level 1

1 Set	**HFL Lying Leg Thrusts**	25 reps (m)	*15 sec. rest*
1 Set	**HFL Lying Leg Thrusts**	20 reps (m)	
1 Set	**Abdominal Crunches**	25 reps (s)	
1 Set	**1/4 Sit-Ups**	10 reps (f)	

Level 2

1 Set	**Hanging Knee-Ups**	10 reps (m)	*15 sec. rest*
1 Set	**Hanging Knee-Ups**	8 reps (m)	
1 Set	**Abdominal Crunches**	25 reps (s)	
1 Set	**Abdominal Crunches**	20 reps (f)	

Level 3

1 Set	**Hanging Knee-Ups**	15 reps (m)	*15 sec. rest*
1 Set	**Hanging Knee-Ups**	10 reps (m)	
1 Set	**HFL Lying Leg Thrusts**	15 reps (s)	
1 Set	**Abdominal Crunches**	20 reps (m)	
1 Set	**1/4 Sit-Ups**	10 reps (f)	

Level 4

1 Set	**Hanging Knee-Ups**	20 reps (m)	*10 sec. rest*
1 Set	**Hanging Knee-Ups**	15 reps (m)	
1 Set	**HFL Lying Leg Thrusts**	20 reps (m)	*10 sec. rest*
1 Set	**HFL Lying Leg Thrusts**	15 reps (m)	
1 Set	**Abdominal Crunches**	30 reps (s)	
1 Set	**1/4 Sit-Ups**	10 reps (f)	

Level 5

1 Set	**Hanging Knee-Ups**	25 reps (m)	*10 sec. rest*
1 Set	**Hanging Knee-Ups**	20 reps (m)	
1 Set	**HFL Lying Leg Thrusts**	20 reps (m)	*10 sec. rest*
1 Set	**HFL Lying Leg Thrusts**	15 reps (m)	
1 Set	**Abdominal Crunches**	35 reps (s)	
1 Set	**1/4 Sit-Ups**	15 reps (f)	

Level 6

1 Set	**Hanging Leg Raises**	5 reps (m)	*10 sec. rest*
1 Set	**Hanging Leg Raises**	5 reps (m)	
1 Set	**Hanging Knee-Ups**	10 reps (m)	
1 Set	**Abdominal Crunches**	35 reps (s)	
1 Set	**1/4 Sit-Ups**	15 reps (f)	

Level 7

1 Set	**Hanging Leg Raises**	10 reps (m)	
1 Set	**Hanging Knee-Ups**	5 reps (m)	*15 sec. rest*
1 Set	**Hanging Leg Raises**	5 reps (m)	
1 Set	**Hanging Knee-Ups**	5 reps (m)	
1 Set	**HFL Lying Leg Thrusts**	25 reps (m)	
1 Set	**Abdominal Crunches**	35 reps (s)	
1 Set	**1/4 Sit-Ups**	15 reps (f)	

Level 8

1 Set	**Hanging Leg Raises**	10 reps (m)	
1 Set	**Hanging Knee-Ups**	5 reps (m)	*10 sec. rest*
1 Set	**Hanging Leg Raises**	10 reps (m)	
1 Set	**Hanging Knee-Ups**	5 reps (m)	
1 Set	**HFL Lying Leg Thrusts**	30 reps (m)	
1 Set	**HFL Lying Leg Thrusts**	25 reps (m)	
1 Set	**Abdominal Crunches**	35 reps (s)	
1 Set	**1/4 Sit-Ups**	15 reps (f)	
1 Set	**Knee Rock-Backs**	15 reps (m)	

Level 9

1 Set	**Hanging Leg Raises**	12 reps (m)	
1 Set	**Hanging Knee-Ups**	as many as possible (m)	*10 sec. rest*
1 Set	**Hanging Leg Raises**	10 reps (m)	
1 Set	**Hanging Knee-Ups**	as many as possible (m)	
1 Set	**HFL Lying Leg Thrusts**	30 reps (m)	*10 sec. rest*
1 Set	**HFL Lying Leg Thrusts**	20 reps (m)	
1 Set	**Cross-Knee Crunches**	as many as possible (s)	
1 Set	**Abdominal Crunches**	as many as possible (m)	
1 Set	**1/4 Sit-Ups**	15 reps (f)	
1 Set	**Knee Rock-Backs**	20 reps (m)	

ILLUSTRATED ROUTINES

To make the routines easier to learn, here they are in pictorial form. These are the same nine levels listed in the previous pages. Follow the general performance guidelines on page 57 concerning speed and advancement through the levels.

Level A

HFL Lying Leg Thrusts
1 set / 15 reps (m) / pg 44

1/4 Sit-Ups
1 set / 25 reps (s) / pg 51

HFL Lying Leg Thrusts
1 set / 10 reps (m) / pg 44

Level 1

HFL Lying Leg Thrusts
1 set / 25 reps (m) / pg 44

HFL Lying Leg Thrusts
1 set / 20 reps (m) / pg 44

Abdominal Crunches
1 set / 25 reps (s) / pg 47

1/4 Sit-Ups
1 set / 20 reps (m) / pg 51

1/4 Sit-Ups
1 set / 10 reps (f) / pg 51

Level 2

Hanging Knee-Ups
1 set / 10 reps (m) / pg 42

Hanging Knee-Ups
1 set / 8 reps (m) / pg 42

Abdominal Crunches
1 set / 25 reps (s) / pg 47

Level 3

Hanging Knee-Ups
1 set / 15 reps (m) / pg 42

Hanging Knee-Ups
1 set / 10 reps (m) / pg 42

HFL Lying Leg Thrusts
1 set / 15 reps (s) / pg 44

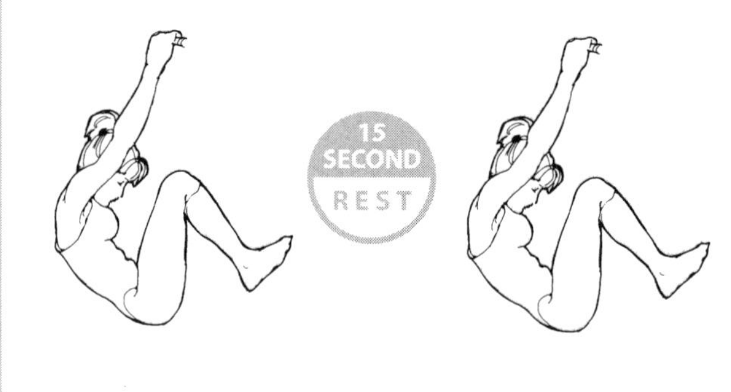

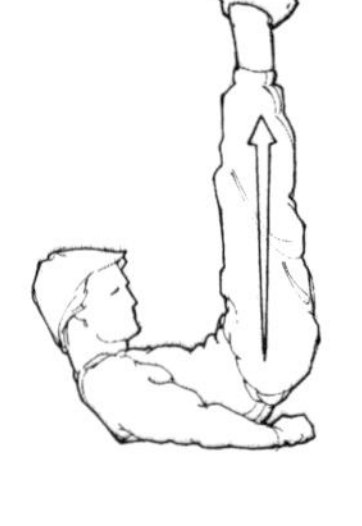

Level 4

Hanging Knee-Ups
1 set / 20 reps (m) / pg 42

Hanging Knee-Ups
1 set / 15 reps (m) / pg 42

HFL Lying Leg Thrusts
1 sets / 20 reps (m) / pg 44

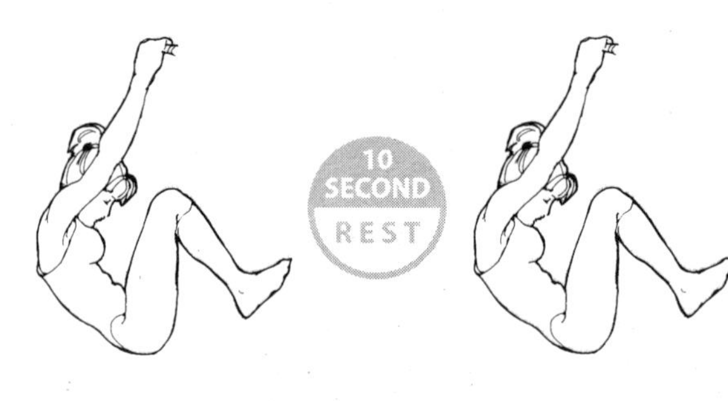

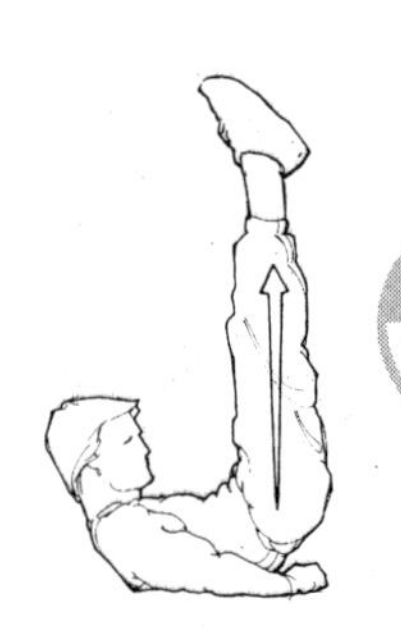

10 SECOND REST

Abdominal Crunches
1 set / 20 reps (f) / pg 47

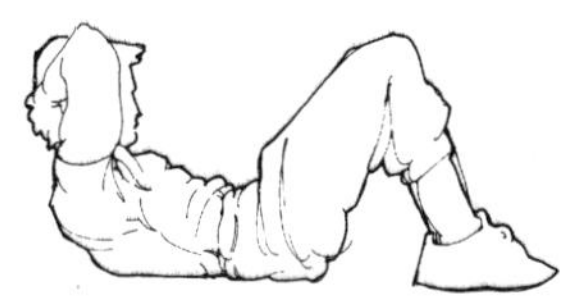

Abdominal Crunches
1 set / 20 reps (m) / pg 47

1/4 Sit-Ups
1 set / 10 reps (f) / pg 51

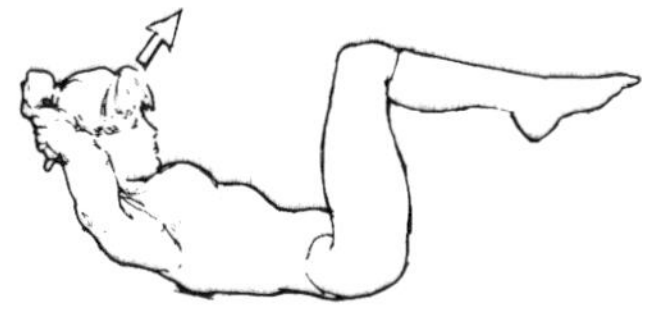

HFL Lying Leg Thrusts
1 set / 15 reps (m) / pg 44

Abdominal Crunches
1 set / 30 reps (s) / pg 47

1/4 Sit-Ups
1 set / 10 reps (f) / pg 51

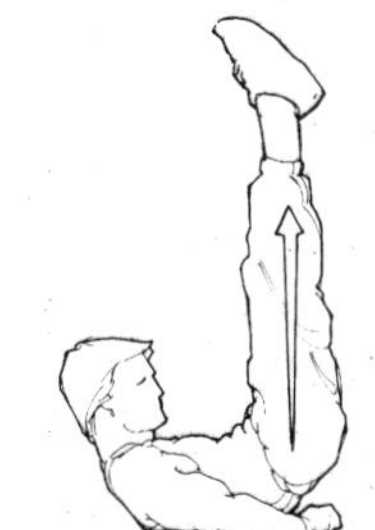

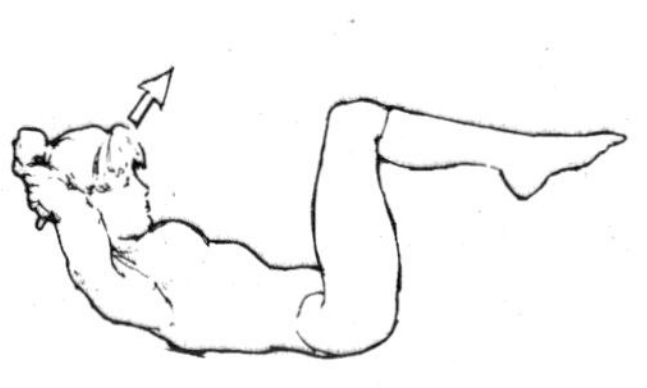

Level 5

Hanging Knee-Ups
1 set / 25 reps (m) / pg 42

Hanging Knee-Ups
1 set / 20 reps (m) / pg 42

HFL Lying Leg Thrusts
1 set / 20 reps (m) / pg 44

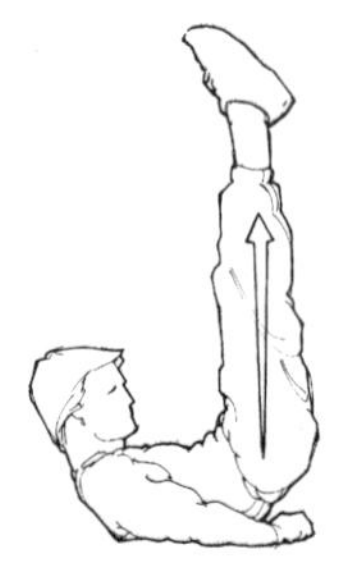

10 SECOND REST

Level 6

Hanging Leg Raises
1 set / 5 reps (m) / pg 40

Hanging Leg Raises
1 set / 5 reps (m) / pg 40

Hanging Knee-Ups
1 set / 10 reps (m) / pg 42

Level 7

Hanging Leg Raises
1 set / 10 reps (m) / pg 40

Hanging Knee-Ups
1 set / 5 reps (m) / pg 42

Hanging Leg Raises
1 set / 5 reps (m) / pg 40

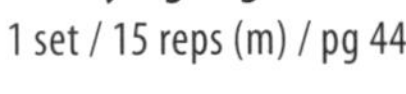

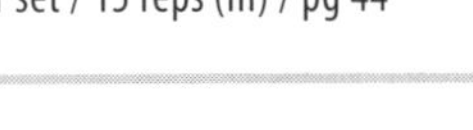

HFL Lying Leg Thrusts
1 set / 15 reps (m) / pg 44

Abdominal Crunches
1 set / 35 reps (s) / pg 47

1/4 Sit-Ups
1 set / 15 reps (f) / pg 51

Abdominal Crunches
1 set / 35 reps (s) / pg 47

1/4 Sit-Ups
1 set / 15 reps (f) / pg 51

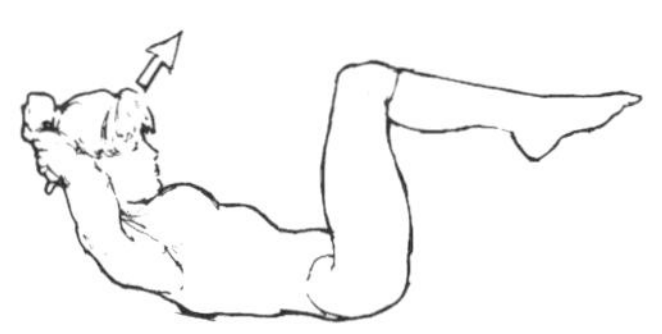

Hanging Knee-Ups
1 set / 5 reps (m) / pg 42

HFL Lying Leg Thrusts
1 set / 25 reps (m) / pg 44

Abdominal Crunches
1 set / 35 reps (s) / pg 47

1/4 Sit-Ups
1 set / 15 reps (f) / pg 51

Level 8

Hanging Leg Raises
1 set / 10 reps (m) / pg 40

Hanging Knee-Ups
1 set / 5 reps (m) / pg 42

Hanging Leg Raises
1 set / 10 reps (m) / pg 40

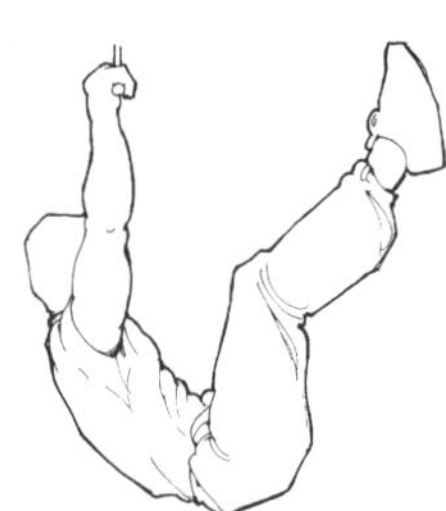

1/4 Sit-Ups
1 set / 15 reps (f) / pg 51

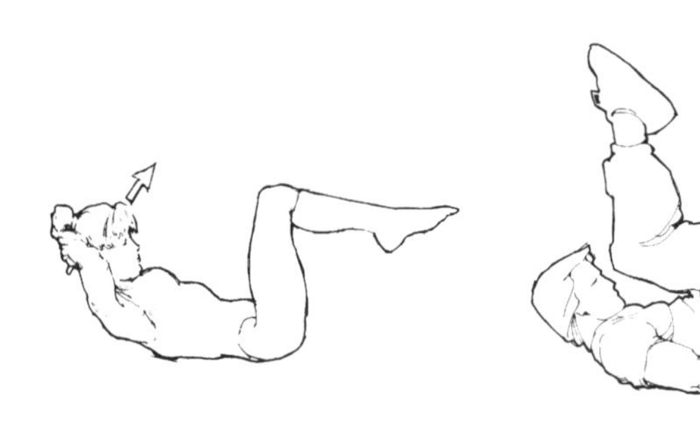

Knee Rock-Backs
1 set / 15 reps (m) / pg 52

Hanging Knee-Ups
1 set / 5 reps (m) / pg 42

HFL Lying Leg Thrusts
1 set / 30 reps (m) / pg 44

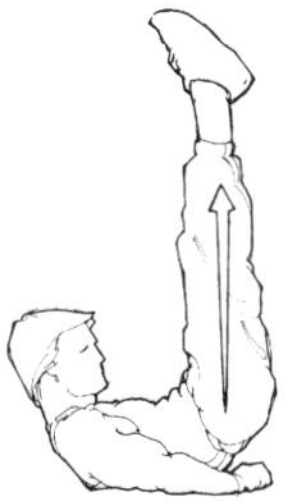

HFL Lying Leg Thrusts
1 set / 25 reps (m) / pg 44

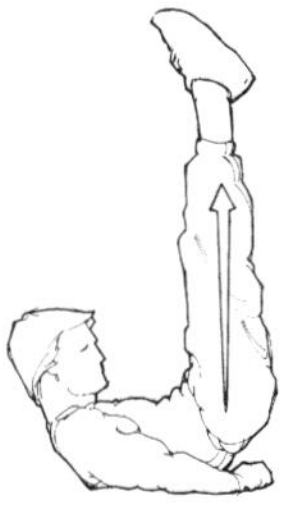

Abdominal Crunches
1 set / 35 reps (s) / pg 47

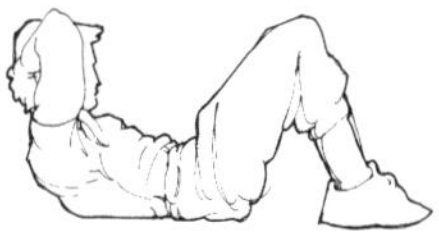

Level 9

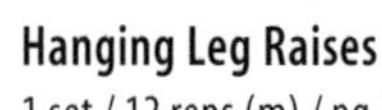

Hanging Leg Raises
1 set / 12 reps (m) / pg 40

Hanging Knee-Ups
1 set as many as possible (m) / pg 42

Hanging Leg Raises
1 set / 10 reps (m) / pg 40

Cross-Knee Crunches
1 set / as many as possible (s) / pg 49

Abdominal Crunches
1 set / as many as possible (s) / pg 47

1/4 Sit-Ups
1 set / 15 reps (f) / pg 51

Hanging Knee-Ups
1 set / as many as possible (m) / pg 42

HFL Lying Leg Thrusts
1 set / 30 reps (m) / pg 44

HFL Lying Leg Thrusts
1 set / 20 reps (m) / pg 44

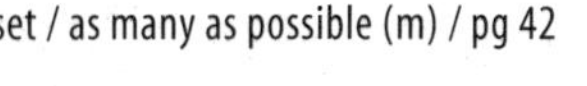

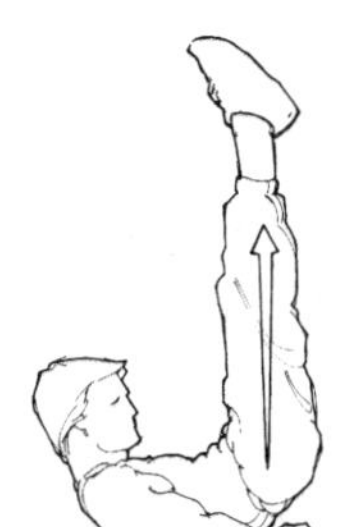

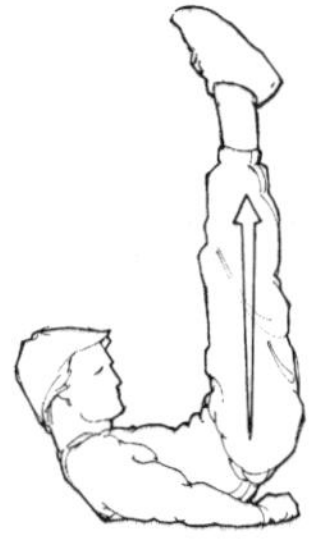

Knee Rock-Backs
1 set / 20 reps (m) / pg 52

How Much, How Often

BEGINNER

If you're new to abdominal training, start at Level A and do the program 3 times per week, with at least one day off between sessions (e.g. M/W/F).

When this gets too easy—and before advancing to Level 1—switch to 4 times per week, grouping workout days in pairs (e.g. M/T, Th/F). You should be able to move up to the next level within a month.

If you wish to add the optional Hyperextensions (see page 56), aim for 1 or 2 sets of 10 to 12 reps. Do these after your back routine, if you do weight-training exercises for your back, or after the *Legendary Abs* routine if you don't.

INTERMEDIATE

Start at Level 1, doing the program 3 days per week with at least one day off between sessions (e.g. M/W/F). When this gets too easy—and before advancing to Level 2—switch to 4 times per week, grouping workout days in pairs (e.g. M/T, Th/F).

If you plan to add the optional Hyperextensions, aim for 2 or 3 sets of 10 to 12 reps. Do these after the *Legendary Abs* routine or after any other work you do for the back muscles.

BEGINNER AND INTERMEDIATE SEQUENCES

START UP

Monday	Wednesday	Friday
Legendary Abs	*Legendary Abs*	*Legendary Abs*

ONGOING

Monday	Tuesday	Wednesday	Thursday	Friday	Saturday
Legendary Abs	*Legendary Abs*	—rest—	*Legendary Abs*	*Legendary Abs*	—rest—

ADVANCED

If you already have been doing extensive training including Hanging Leg Raises done with correct form (see page 40), start at Level 7 or 8, training 4 days per week, grouped in pairs (e.g. M/T, Th/F). If you have access to a lat pull-down machine, add 2 sets of Pull-Down Ab Crunches on the first day of each pair.

Perform Hyperextensions following your normal back work or following *Legendary Abs* on any "non-back" days.

ADVANCED SEQUENCE

STANDARD

Monday	Tuesday	Wednesday	Thursday	Friday	Saturday
Legendary Abs	*Legendary Abs*	—rest—	*Legendary Abs*	*Legendary Abs*	—rest—
Pull-Down Ab Crunches			Pull-Down Ab Crunches		

WITH 5-DAY/3-WEEK ROUTINE FROM
Secrets of Advanced Bodybuilders, Supplement #1

Monday	Tuesday	Wednesday	Thursday	Friday	Saturday
Legendary Abs	*Legendary Abs*	no abs	—rest—	*Legendary Abs*	*Legendary Abs*

With this schedule, do Pull-Down Crunches on the same days you work lower body.

Fat Loss: Key to Definition

In Chapter 1, we covered the toning of abdominal muscle. This chapter deals with another aspect of ab training: **definition**. Definition refers to how clearly your abs stand out—how chiseled, or *cut*, they appear. Definition depends largely on how much bodyfat you have. Male or female, the more fat there is covering your abs, the less defined they'll be.

Many people hope the same exercises that build their abs will also "spot reduce" fat from their waist. They may do hundreds of sit-ups or crunches a week and wonder why they still have a bulge. Unfortunately, no matter how much ab training you do, it won't take fat off your waist. And, no matter how toned your abs get, you're never going to have that tight-looking washboard until you lose any excess fat that's covering the muscle.

4

FAT LOSS FOR DEFINITION

In this chapter, we'll show you how to combine certain kinds of exercise with special dietary modifications in a way *guaranteed* to give you results, even if you've had trouble trimming down in the past.

Maybe you're someone who's spent years alternately dieting and backsliding—watching your weight fluctuate 20 pounds or more. Or maybe you've never had a weight problem before, but now you've hit your mid-30's and suddenly you're carrying around a little paunch that didn't used to be there. Either way, this approach will work for you.

A Starting Point

Part of the difficulty in trying to lose weight is the constant bombardment from the media promoting this or that new "revolutionary" solution. Common sense should tell us that if fat took years to accumulate, it's not going to melt away overnight. Still, it's easy to be taken in—dramatic promises of weight loss are more compelling than the prospect of disciplined work.

We're going to bypass the hype and take a step-by-step, scientific approach, based on the realities of human physiology. Even if you think you've heard it all before, read on! Even though there are no miracles when it comes to weight loss, there *are* very specific guidelines that will help you get the most out of your effort. Specifically, this chapter will unveil the *Legendary Abs* High-Low Nutritional Plan—based on a never-before published technique for losing fat *without* the risks and pitfalls of traditional diets.

With the High-Low Plan, you'll be able not only to *take* it off, but *keep* it off—and you'll do it without huge sacrifices. Just follow the plan step by step, and you'll be on the road to getting the firm, tight, and *well-defined* abs you've always wanted.

The Energy Equation

The problem of excess fat centers around the subject of *energy*, specifically the balance of energy *in vs.* energy *out*.

ENERGY IN

Your body requires a constant supply of energy. That energy comes from the breakdown of a potent chemical called **adenosine triphosphate**, or **ATP.**

ATP is the high-test gasoline of the human engine. Yet, at any given time, your body only contains about 3 ounces of ATP, roughly enough for a 6-second sprint. To sustain exertion, your body must fuel itself by continuously creating new ATP. It does this by **metabolizing**, or breaking down, glucose and fat molecules drawn from the carbohydrates and fat in your diet. (A small amount of the protein you eat is also converted to glucose and becomes ATP, but most is used to maintain muscle mass and perform myriad other functions.)

The energy potential of the nutrients we consume is measured in **calories.*** When broken down by our body, each gram of protein produces 4 calories of energy; each gram of carbohydrate, 4 calories; and each gram of fat, *a whopping 9 calories.*

CALORIC EXPENDITURE (ENERGY OUT)

Just being alive burns calories. The various processes of breathing, circulation, digestion, and so on, require anywhere from 1,000 to 2,000 calories a day. The amount of energy your body needs just to function normally is your **basal metabolic rate,** the rate at which it consumes fuel while at rest. Any physical activity, of course, burns additional calories.

The combination of your basal metabolic rate plus energy demands created by physical activity is your total **caloric expenditure**. An average adult man expends about 2,000 calories of energy every day; an average adult woman, about 1,800 calories.

Any calories you consume over that number are converted to bodyfat.

* One calorie is the amount of energy required to heat 1 gram of water 1 degree Celcius.

Ideally, energy in should equal energy out. If it does, your weight remains constant. For most of us, though, this energy equation doesn't always balance. One of the reasons is that as we get older—usually in our 30's—our basal metabolic rate slows in response to hormonal changes. Our bodies burn fewer calories. Yet we don't adjust our eating accordingly, and we begin to develop a surplus of calories. This effect is intensified by the fact that most of us become less physically active as we get older, lowering our caloric expenditure even further. Little by little, more calories are coming in than are going out, and the excess ends up in fat cells.

Calorie Deficit

The only solution is to reverse the process—to adjust your consumption and expenditure so that you burn more calories than you take in. This creates what's called a **calorie deficit**. Once in a state of calorie deficit, your body will begin to draw on stored carbohydrate and fat. Gradually, the fat stores shrink and your weight goes down.

This doesn't happen overnight. Fat is a very efficient fuel, capable of producing *lots* of ATP. A single pound of fat contains about 3,500 calories of stored energy. To lose it, you're going to have to somehow create a 3,500 calorie deficit.

The question is: *How?*

The Dieting Dilemma

You probably already knew, even before reading the last section, that eating more calories than you use results in fat gain. What many of us overlook is that the problem is not calorie consumption per se, it's the *imbalance* between calorie intake and expenditure. When people focus only on the "calories in" part of the equation, they end up trying to remedy the problem with **dieting**—that is, severely reducing their caloric intake for a brief period of time.

WHY DIETS DON'T WORK

Common sense should tell us that if any of the popular diets actually *worked*—that is, allowed you to remove fat "overnight" and keep it off forever—then America's vast diet industry would disappear. This obviously hasn't happened, nor is it going to. The fact is, there are some basic reasons no crash diet can ever work.

One problem, as mentioned above, is that dieting is a lopsided solution. Calorie consumption is only one-half of the energy equation. Dieting without exercising is like trying to fix a stopped drain by shutting off the water supply to the faucet.

Another problem with dieting is the underlying idea that it's possible to lose weight *fast.* ("Lose 10 pounds in two weeks!") But chances are your body didn't *gain* the weight fast. Think about it: Most of us keep a fairly steady weight until we approach middle age. At that point, our metabolism naturally slows and we start to put on a couple of pounds each year. After five years or so, we decide impulsively to do something about it. Yet we expect to fix the problem in a matter of weeks.

When you try to lose weight fast, and you only employ calorie restriction to do it, several problems occur, including loss of muscle, metabolic slowdown, and diminished health and well-being.

Loss of Muscle

Any weight you lose through dietary restriction alone will be composed almost equally of fat and lean tissue. While most stored energy resides in the form of fat, you also have a lot of energy stored in the form of muscle protein. Unless you are placing demands on your muscles by exercising, your body will begin to burn that protein for energy. So all the time you're losing fat, you'll be losing muscle too.

This is bad, for two reasons: First, although you may end up looking thinner, you'll have lost the lean mass that gives the body shape and makes you look fit. Second, since your muscles provide one of the main ways to *use* energy, less muscle means even less caloric expenditure. When you eventually go off the diet, your body is even more susceptible to gaining weight than it was before.

Metabolic Slowdown

Severe caloric restriction slows the basal metabolism. Sudden drops in caloric intake set off an alarm in your body called the **starvation response.** This is an adaptive mechanism, left over from a time in evolutionary history when food shortages were a threat to survival. A signal goes out that says, "Hey, slow down! The tank's nearly empty!"

When you diet, you are essentially starving yourself. Your body responds accordingly by lowering its basal metabolism to conserve energy. Now you're eating fewer calories, but you're also *burning* fewer calories. The net result is that there's little or no calorie deficit. You don't lose any fat—you just end up feeling listless and frustrated.

In fact, any reduction in daily calorie consumption by more than about 15% will cause your metabolism to slow down almost the same amount in response.

Diminished Health and Well-Being

Of course, if you cut your caloric intake drastically enough, you will lose weight. After all, you're starving! Your body must somehow produce the basic energy to function, and there's a limit to how far it can lower its basal metabolism. But even mild starvation isn't good for you. It disrupts your body chemistry, makes you susceptible to illness, and leaves you feeling tired and hungry.

As anyone who has dieted knows, the net effect of most diets is that you lose weight for only a short time. Once you stop the diet, your body responds to the starvation mechanism by seeking out all those calories it was missing. Most diets are followed by a slow, steady binge that leaves you even heavier than before.

Summary

- Crash dieting results in a loss of lean muscle tissue and slowdown of metabolism, making it even easier to gain weight once you go off the diet.
- Dieting inevitably creates a yo-yo effect of weight loss followed by weight gain.
- Lowering your caloric intake by more than 15% results in a corresponding drop in basal metabolic rate.

An Integrated Approach

The fact is, dietary measures alone simply don't work. What *does* work is the integration of reasonable, moderate eating with a moderate level of exercise. *Regular* exercise not only burns calories, but it helps minimize the amount of muscle mass you lose during weight loss. *Vigorous* exercise stimulates muscle growth and deters your body from consuming its muscle protein as energy. Exercise also causes hormonal changes that make it easier to retrieve stored fat for energy fuel.

Together, the two components of exercise and sensible eating work synergistically to promote a *healthful* lifestyle—with minimal bodyfat as a prime benefit. In the next two sections we'll discuss these two components and offer guidelines (including the *Legendary Abs* High-Low Schedule) to help you combine them for best results.

Exercise for Fat Loss

As we have seen, exercise is a key part of the task of rebalancing your caloric intake and expenditure.

There are two ways to create a calorie deficit through exercise:

- by using **aerobic exercise** to burn calories
- by using **strength exercise** to increase muscle mass

Aerobic exercise has a direct effect on fat by drawing on energy stores to support the activity itself. Depending on how vigorously you exercise, it may also stimulate muscle growth to some degree.

Strength exercise leads to fat loss by increasing the mass of your muscles. Each pound of additional muscle on your frame raises your basal metabolic rate, enabling you to burn more calories all the time—even at rest.

AEROBIC EXERCISE

Creating a caloric deficit through aerobic exercise is a function of three things: exercise **duration**, **intensity**, and **frequency**. The *longer* and *harder* you exercise, the more energy you burn. The more *frequently* you exercise, the more energy you burn over time.

How long and hard will you need to exercise? The simple guideline is: *the more calories you burn, the better.* Whether you exercise at high intensity for a short time or low intensity for a long time doesn't really matter—theoretically, at least. But practically speaking, you are most likely to succeed in the long run by taking the middle road.

Here's why:

The Intensity/Duration Trade-off

Clearly, there's a limit to how much you can push yourself to exercise both harder *and* longer. Because of the way your body produces energy, it's almost impossible to do highly intense exercise for a long period. And although you can get pretty fit by doing intense *short*-duration exercise, it's hard to lose weight that way. Losing fat requires burning many calories, and short duration exercise rarely burns enough calories in total.

Long-duration *low*-intensity exercise, on the other hand, while effective, is time consuming.* Since most of us don't have the luxury of devoting huge amounts of time to our physical training, this is an important consideration.

For maximum calorie burning, it's usually better to exercise at a *moderate intensity* for a *moderately* long duration.

*Although it's true that very prolonged, low-intensity exercise draws the highest possible percentage of energy from fat stores, the difference is not significant in the context of general weight loss. You'll burn more calories overall—and therefore more total fat calories—by doing higher intensity exercise. In addition, higher intensity exercise is more likely to build muscle mass, which will help raise your basal metabolism to burn calories even when you're resting.

Moderate Intensity

What is *moderate intensity?* In practical terms, it means whatever intensity level you can *sustain* for at least 30–45 minutes. This is long enough to create a meaningful calorie deficit, hopefully without imposing unreasonable time demands.

It's important to note that aerobic exercise for weight reduction should be *less* intense than that for cardiovascular conditioning. Cardiovascular training is best done for shorter periods (approximately 20–30 minutes) at a level just below the **lactic threshold** (about 70–80% of your maximum heart rate*). At this level, you should be just barely able to carry on a conversation.

The best intensity for weight management, however, is 60–70% of your maximum heart rate. At this level, you should be breaking a light sweat and should be able to converse easily—and even to sing.

Ramping Up

What if you're very unfit to start? In this case, almost any exercise will seem very intense. Initially, you may not be able to exercise long enough at any intensity level to burn a significant number of calories. Your first goal should be to acquire a basic level of fitness. Your initial exercise program should consist of several short bouts of exercise with rest intervals. Do this for several weeks until you become fit enough to train for longer periods.

Your goal should be to develop the stamina needed to exercise continuously for at least 30–45 minutes. Then, gradually increase the intensity of your workouts. Only when you can train with pretty good intensity for 45 minutes should you try lengthening the duration of your workouts if you want more calorie burn.

*To figure your maximum heart rate: (For a man) 220 - age = MHR; (For a woman) 227 - age = MHR

What Type of Aerobic Exercise Should You Do?

1. **Make sure the exercise you choose can be sustained for up to 45 minutes.** As we've explained, burning fat requires medium-to-long-duration continuous exercise. Doing twenty 6-second sprints may tire you out, and even improve your sprinting ability, but it won't do much to burn fat. After all, it's only 2 minutes of exercise. Ideally, you should train for at least 30 minutes, with 45 minutes as a recommended initial goal. If you're already fit and want to burn more calories, just increase the duration or intensity of your training.

2. **Choose a form of exercise you enjoy.** Grinding out 5 miles a day if you hate running will only make you dread your daily workouts. If you're fond of an activity that doesn't lend itself to calorie burning, try to find ways to increase the intensity level. If you love to pay golf, for example, the only way you'll really burn many calories is to forego the motorized cart, sling your clubs over your shoulder, and walk the course carrying those extra 20 pounds. In some cases, you may have to supplement your favorite sport with another form of exercise, but in the end, doing what you enjoy will keep you going.

3. **If possible, choose weight-bearing exercises.** Research shows that weight-bearing exercises such as running or cross-county skiing burn more calories than non-weight bearing exercise. This does not mean that swimming and cycling are bad choices, especially if you enjoy them, but they are less efficient calorie-burners than some other activities.

Best choices:

- Brisk walking
- Hiking (specifically uphill)
- Running
- Jumping rope
- Cross-country skiing
- Treadmill
- In-line skating
- Stair climbing
- Aerobic dance (low impact)

Second best:

- Cycling
- Spinning
- Swimming
- Rowing

Here are some more examples of the caloric expenditure of various exercises:

Calories burned per hour, assuming bodyweight of 160 lbs.	
Volleyball	219
Treading water (slow)	272
Walking (3 mph)	276
Cycling (5.5 mph)	280
Tennis	477
In-line skating	329
Walking (4 mph)	412
Cycling (9.4 mph)	438
Swimming (slow crawl)	561
Running (11-minute mile)	591
Basketball	604
Swimming (fast crawl)	683
Running (9-minute mile)	845
Running (6-minute mile)	1104
Chopping wood (fast)	1301

STRENGTH TRAINING

Resistance training with weights can be a valuable addition to your weight-loss effort. While aerobic exercise burns calories during the activity itself, resistance training aimed at strength building leads to changes in your body that let you burn more calories all the time. Each pound of muscle you gain raises your basal metabolic rate by about 50 calories a day. Ten pounds of new muscle on your frame would consume an extra 3,500 calories a week *just by being there.*

By doing aerobic exercise along with a small amount of resistance exercise aimed at strength building, you'll be hitting your weight problem from two sides at once and promoting faster results.

We're not talking about trying to develop the extreme muscularity of the bodybuilder. Ten pounds of muscle, distributed on the frame of a 160-pound man, will not create an impression of extreme muscularity—it will simply make him look fit.

Basic Resistance Training Guidelines

For complete resistance training guidelines, see *Secrets of Advanced Bodybuilders,* published by *Health For Life,* which offers complete weight-training programs for people at all levels. The bottom line is that *any* amount of resistance training will be beneficial. Here are some general guidelines:

- Do 6–8 reps per set, with 45-second rests between sets.
- Do no more than 10 sets for any one major bodypart (chest, back, etc.)
- Do no more than 5–7 sets for any one minor bodypart (biceps, triceps, etc.)
- Keep your strength training workout under 1 hour total.
- Train your whole body 3 times a week, or split upper and lower body into separate workouts and do each twice a week (4-day split workouts should be no more than about 45 minutes each).

Summary

- Calorie-burning depends on exercise intensity, duration, and frequency.
- *Best bet:* exercise at moderate intensity, which is the level you can sustain for a minimum of 30–45 minutes (ideally, 60–70% of your maximum heart rate).
- Resistance training will accelerate your weight-loss efforts by building new muscle, which in turn raises your basal metabolism.

Eating Right

It wasn't long ago, in terms of human evolution, that it made sense to eat as much as possible. After all, food wasn't always abundant and you never knew when you'd eat again. Our problem occurs when we indulge this primal urge in a world where food is plentiful—especially since most of us are far less active than our prehistoric ancestors.

Maintaining the weight you want shouldn't require any sort of drastic measures. It does require eating the right *types* of food, eating the right *amount* of food, and exercising consistently. We've already discussed exercise; now we'll focus on the details of a dietary program that will allow you to create a calorie deficit without the ups and downs of traditional dieting.

THE LEGENDARY ABS HIGH-LOW PLAN

As you recall, one of the problems of most diets is that a calorie deficit of more than 300 per day is enough to trigger the body's starvation response, thereby lowering your basal metabolism and partially negating the deficit.

The *Legendary Abs* fat reduction approach is based on consuming just *slightly* fewer calories than your daily requirement. In addition, it uses the *Legendary Abs* High-Low Schedule, a technique that recent studies have shown helps further guard against metabolic slowdown. By combining *moderate caloric restriction* with the increased calorie demands of *regular exercise,* you should be able to lose body fat without triggering the body's starvation response.

The larger part of the calorie deficit will come from the exercise you do. Nevertheless, the specific dietary guidelines of the High-Low plan are critical to the plan's success.

By this method, you'll be able to lose about a pound or two of fat a week. (In fact, losing more than 1% of your bodyweight per week would result in a loss of lean tissue.) Do that for just 10 weeks, however, and you'll lose at least 10 pounds!

The basic dietary guidelines are…

1. **Limit the amount of fat you eat.** The mere presence of fats in the bloodstream triggers enzymatic activity around your fat cells that predispose them to store fat more efficiently. Limiting your fat intake has the opposite effect—fat cell metabolism shifts its emphasis away from fat storage and your body prepares to *retrieve* fat from the cells for use in energy production.

   Authorities disagree on the amount of fat you should eat. Recommendations range from Pritikin's very austere 10% to as much as 30% at the high end of the American Medical Association's range. Since the average American's diet is nearly 40% fat, anywhere in the 10 to 30% range would be a significant improvement. To help smooth the transition to healthier eating, we suggest dropping initially to 30% and then gradually lowering the percentage over a period of months until you find the lowest level you can live with comfortably.

As much as possible, choose unsaturated fats. (Unsaturated fats come from vegetable sources and are liquid at room temperature.) They are stored less readily than saturated fats, and do not have the detrimental effect on blood cholesterol levels that saturated fats do.

2. **Restrict your intake by *no more than* 200 to 300 cal/day.** This is the most you can cut back without triggering the starvation response and slowing your metabolism. (Note: This is assuming a daily intake of about 2,000 cal/day. If your current intake is much higher, you can cut a little more. If it is closer to 3,000, cut 300–400 cal/day.)

3. **Follow the High-Low Schedule.** Because everyone's body responds differently, just keeping your calorie restriction below 300 calories doesn't guarantee you won't slow your metabolism. That's why we've developed the *Legendary Abs* High-Low Schedule of caloric restriction. Here's how it works:

   Recent nutritional studies have shown that you can further guard against metabolic slowdown by *alternating days of greater and lesser calorie restriction.* For example, if you wanted to cut your intake by an average of 200 calories per day, you would alternate days of 100-calorie restriction with days of 300-calorie restriction. This would average out, over the long run, to a 200-calorie drop.

   Without the High-Low Schedule, a 200-calorie drop *could* trigger the body's starvation response and slow its basal metabolism. But because the High-Low Schedule calls for interspersing days when the calorie restriction is slight (only 100 calories), the body doesn't react to the overall reduction that's occurring. Your metabolism stays up and you get the benefit of the calorie deficit.

   To implement the High-Low Schedule, first determine your present caloric intake. The best way to do this is to keep a food diary. Without changing your diet, simply write down everything you eat for one week, total up the calories and divide by 7 to get your daily average.* If your present intake is around 2000 calories, create a schedule based on an average reduction of 200-calorie/day: On day 1, restrict 300 calories; on day 2 restrict 100 calories; on day 3, restrict 300 calories, and so on.

   Here's a sample schedule, showing how to create an average 200-calorie deficit from a baseline of 2,000 calories day:

Sample High-Low Schedule	
Day 1	1700 calories
Day 2	1900 calories
Day 3	1700 calories
Day 4	1900 calories
Day 5	1700 calories
Day 6	1900 calories
Day 7	1700 calories
(continue alternating)	
Average calorie intake for the week: 1800/day	
Average calorie deficit (assuming 2000 cal/day baseline) 200 cal/day	

WHAT TO EXPECT

Together, the High-Low method and regular exercise make it relatively easy to lose a pound or two per week. *How much you actually lose will depend on how much you exercise.* To get the fat-loss benefits of exercise, you should do *at least* 30–45 minutes of aerobic weight-bearing exercise, 4 times per week at the highest intensity you can sustain. That amount of exercise will create an energy demand of 1600–2400 calories per week, depending on the intensity you achieve. When you combine the exercise calorie expenditure with the weekly deficit of 1200–1400 calories you get from restricting your intake, you will achieve a total caloric deficit of approximately 3000–4000 calories.

If you can exercise 5 or 6 days a week and increase the length or intensity of your sessions, you will lose even more. Doing resistance exercise to develop additional muscle mass will also accelerate your results.

* There are many good reference books available that provide calorie figures for hundreds of foods. Two of the best are the *Corine T. Netzer Encyclopedia of Food Values,* Dell Publishing, NY; and *Food Values of Portions Commonly Used,* by Pennington & Church, Harper Row, NY.

Summary: Fat Loss at a Glance

Here again are the general guidelines for maximizing your potential for fat loss. Because of the variables involved—types of exercise, intensity levels, individual metabolisms, stress, sleep, etc.—it's impossible to design a precise plan that will be appropriate for everyone—nor is it necessary to plot your life to the last calorie. If you stay within the framework presented here, you can fine tune your intake and expenditure as you go.

- **Plan to lose a *maximum* of 1–2 pounds or 1% of your total bodyweight per week.** Additional weight loss comes from lean body mass, not fat. The deficit necessary to lose 1 to 2 lbs is 3500–7000 cal/week, or 500–1000 cal/day.
- **Restrict your calorie intake an average of 200–300 cal/day *maximum*** according to the *Legendary Abs* High-Low Schedule, alternating days of eating at 100-150 calories below your baseline requirement with days at 300-450 below baseline.
- **Restrict your fat intake.** Limit your intake of saturated fats as much as possible, and limit your consumption of fats in general to no more than 30% of your diet at first, gradually working down to 10–20%.
- **Create the remainder of the needed deficit through exercise, averaging a 200–700 cal/day expenditure.** This would be equivalent to walking or running 2 to 6 miles, or doing 30–45 minutes of moderate-intensity exercise, a day. On low caloric intake days, your energy expenditure need not be as great—walking 2 to 3 miles or the equivalent is adequate. On high caloric intake days you can do more intense aerobic activity, such as running, cycling, aerobics, spinning, in-line skating, or similar activities.

KEEPING THE WEIGHT OFF

Once you've reached your desired weight, you can begin to modify this regimen a bit. You'll still need to exercise and watch your calorie intake, but you can be a little less strict. Likewise, don't fret if you have to miss a workout because your schedule gets overly hectic. Just don't let it turn into a week or two (or three) of no exercise. Keep in mind that if you start building a calorie surplus, you'll gain back those pounds.

PUTTING IT ALL TOGETHER

We've now got the elements that work together to build the ultimate set of firm, well-defined abs:

- The *Legendary Abs* Workout (6 minutes, 3 to 4 times/week)
- Aerobic training (4 to 6 times/week)
- Strength training—*optional, but recommended* (3 to 4 times/week)
- Legendary Abs High-Low Schedule of caloric intake (alternating days)

As far as how to schedule your abdominal conditioning, aerobic exercise, and days of restricted caloric intake, there's no better or worse combination. It doesn't matter whether you do your aerobic exercise on a normal or a restricted eating day because the caloric reduction is so slight. Many people, however, do their abdominal conditioning on the same days they weight train.

Sample Schedule

Here's just one example of how these elements might be put together. Using this schedule, Sunday would be a rest day and would continue the high-low alternation sequence. (Notice that since high and low calorie restriction days alternate, "high" and "low" days won't fall on the same days of the week two weeks in a row.)

Monday	Tuesday	Wednesday	Thursday	Friday	Saturday
HIGH	*LOW*	*HIGH*	*LOW*	*HIGH*	*LOW*
Abs Strength tr.		*Abs* Strength tr.	—rest—	*Abs* Strength tr.	
Aerobic tr.	Aerobic tr.	Aerobic tr.		Aerobic tr.	Aerobic tr.

If you do strength training, we recommend doing it *before* aerobic work on days when you do both. Strength training helps use up stored glycogen so that the aerobic work will draw more fuel from fat.

One final point: Since weight training does use mostly glycogen for energy, it tends to stimulate your appetite. On strength training days, you may experience food cravings due to low blood sugar. We recommend a post-workout snack of some fruit or fructose-containing food to counteract any blood sugar drop, and help prevent overeating.

Psychological Factors

In this chapter, we've approached weight loss in a purely mechanistic way—as through the body was simply a fuel burning engine. Of course, the reality is more complex. The body and mind are closely and mysteriously linked.

In many cases, there are psychological reasons for people's weight problems—factors that may induce them to overeat and neglect their health. These factors can be very subtle and difficult to resolve. Often a person is unable to put a weight loss plan into practice without first addressing the underlying causes of the problem.

We've tried to present a simple, straightforward plan that should be easy to follow and obtain results. Nevertheless, our plan does require disciplined work. If you find you are unable to stick to the plan, but you're still troubled by excess weight, you might consider seeking professional counseling to help you explore the roots of, and possible solutions to the problem.

❖ ❖ ❖

Losing weight need not entail huge sacrifices. In just a few months of exercising regularly and eating sensibly, you can feel better, have greater strength and stamina, and, of course, build a set of abs that look like they're going to jump through your skin! All it takes is a moderate, consistent effort. Good luck!

CHAPTER 4

FAT LOSS FOR DEFINITION

Training for Athletic Power

We've all heard professional and Olympic athletes recount grueling training regimens that may include hundreds, if not thousands, of sit-ups or "abs." Although such claims are usually creative exaggerations to give these athletes a superhuman air, performance athletes *do* need more abdominal training than somebody who just wants to look good at the beach.

5

AB TRAINING FOR ATHLETIC POWER

Being athletically strong, however, doesn't mean doing thousands of sit-ups. As explained in Chapter 1, most high-rep abdominal conditioning is inefficient, even potentially dangerous. In this section, we'll take a look at how to train your abs for optimum athletic performance, without wasted effort or risk. By combining the basic *Legendary Abs* program with some additional exercises to address the specific demands of athletic performance, you can develop great-looking abs that also pack a punch out on the playing field.

Performance Benefits of Strong Abs

Here's a little secret that many athletes, professionals included, just don't know: *Strong abdominals are one of the keys to great athletic performance.*

How can that be? After all, you don't run or jump with your abs. You don't throw, shoot or swing with them either. So why are abs so important?

The truth is, you *do* run, jump, and throw from your abs. The torso, (also referred to as the **trunk,** or **pillar**) is a crucial component of the sequential movements that make up any athletic activity. Sports scientists call this sequence of coordinated muscle movements the **kinetic chain.** And the abdominal muscles are the center links of that chain.

FORCE TRANSFER & STABILITY

How does the kinetic chain work? Well, for most sports, the large muscle groups of your legs generate most of the force and energy. In a baseball swing, for example, the power originates in your legs and must be transferred to your arms (and ultimately to the bat) through your torso (Fig. 5-1). For your swing to develop much force, your torso must provide a stable, yet flexible, conduit that will allow the energy from your legs to travel to the end of the bat.

Every time you swing a tennis racquet, hit a baseball, jump for a rebound, or catch a football, your torso muscles—especially your abs—are hard at work. If those muscles aren't strong enough, your performance suffers. The kinetic chain is only as strong as its weakest link.

Fig.5-1 Force travels from the legs, through hip rotation, through the trunk, to the bat.

Let's say you have to move a heavy rock, only you're not allowed to touch it. You have a choice of two tools: a strong wooden pole and a section of flexible rubber hose. Which is the better tool for the job? The wooden pole, of course, because when you push the rock with the pole, it moves easily. If you try the same with the rubber hose, the hose bends and the rock goes nowhere. Because the hose isn't strong and stable, you can't transfer the force you produce to the rock. That's exactly how your abs work when it comes to athletic performance. So, you have a choice. Your abs can be like a strong pillar or they can be like that soft rubber hose.

Fig. 5-2 Lead jab—over 70% of the force originates in the legs and trunk.

Take another example: a straight right jab. On the face of it, you might assume that most of the force of a punch comes from the muscles of the arm and shoulder. But in fact, a full 76% of the force of a good jab originates in the legs and trunk (Fig. 5-2). Once again, the abs serve as a conduit—enabling the force to travel up through the kinetic chain to the fist.

These examples illustrate how crucial a strong torso—meaning strong abs—is to physical performance. The stronger and more stable your trunk is, the more efficiently your effort is translated into action.

MOVEMENTS OF THE TRUNK

Besides providing a stable trunk through which to transfer force, strong abdominal muscles also generate considerable force of their own. Almost every sport involves several different trunk movements, including bending forward, backward, and to the side, as well as twisting. Understanding how the abs move the torso and how this, in turn, contributes to athletic power, will help you get the most out of training for athletics.

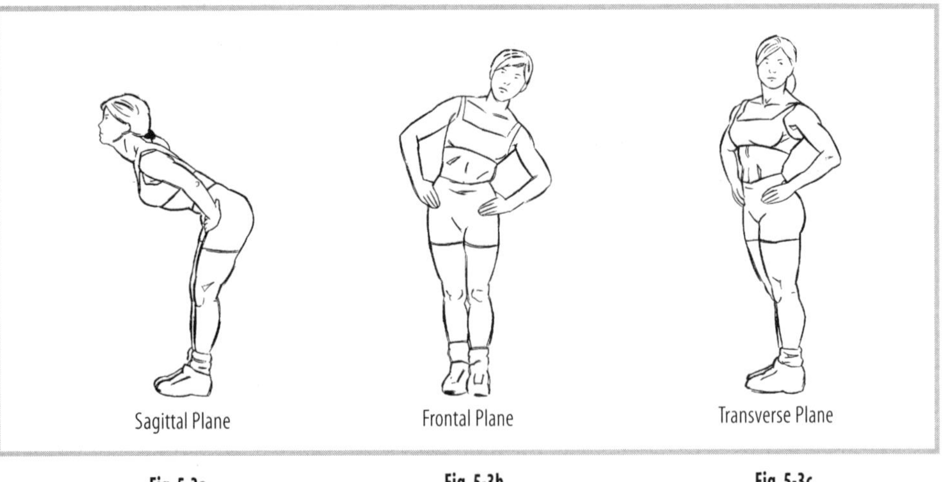

Fig. 5-3a **Fig. 5-3b** **Fig. 5-3c**

Remember from Chapters 1 and 2 that there are four groups of abdominal muscles: the rectus abdominis (composed of upper and lower abs), the internal and external obliques and the transversalis. Associated with these are the psoas muscles, which, though not part of the abdominal group, play a role in forward bending of the torso. The psoas is one of a group of muscles known as the hip flexors, a group that also includes the rectus femoris, of the quadriceps. Hip flexor strength is an key component of athletic power.

Fig. 5-4a Fig. 5-4b Fig. 5-4c

These muscles work together to generate force in the many positions required by different sports. The upper and lower abs are responsible for flexing the spine and protecting it during extension. The external obliques are primarily responsible for bending to the side and twisting. The internal obliques help twist the torso and stabilize the spine, as does the transversalis. The hip flexors enable jackknife-like motions at the hip.

Each of these muscles groups helps the torso move through one or more of its three **planes of motion.** Side-to-side bending occurs in the **sagittal** plane (Fig. 5-3a). Forward and backward bending occurs in the **frontal** plane (Fig. 5-3b). Rotation (twisting left or right) occurs in the **transverse** plane (Fig. 5-3c). Usually, during sports, the torso moves through more than one plane at the same time: you flex while twisting; you bend while flexing, and so on. This requires a coordinated interaction of the muscles.

It is part of the miraculous design of the abs that they are able to act as the stable pillar described earlier, while at the same time flexing and rotating the trunk to contribute additional force of their own.

Imagine a baseball pitcher in the act of releasing a pitch. He initiates the throw by driving with his legs (Fig. 5-4a). This force is transferred through the trunk toward the shoulder and arm. At the same time, the torso (which started out rotated and hyperextended backward) rotates and flexes forward, adding force to the pitch. (Fig. 5-4b,c). Nearly all the abdominal muscles are involved in this stabilizing, flexing, and rotating of the torso. Imagine how hard and with what precise coordination the abdominal muscles must work to enable a major leaguer to hurl a 95 mph fastball over the plate!

Such total abdominal involvement is the rule in athletic performance. Think of your own favorite sport. If it involves throwing or hitting, the example just given pretty accurately describes what happens. If you're a martial artist, similar things happen. Every punch requires a large contribution from the abdomen. The entire trunk rotates and moves forward, requiring explosive action of the obliques and upper abs. Every roundhouse kick calls on the obliques, lower abs, and hip flexors to pull the leg around. No matter what your sport, your abs are always working.

Weak Lower Abs

Many athletes who have a well-defined stomach actually have very weak lower abs. We've seen many cases of elite marathon runners who can't even do a single good lying leg thrust. Often, the culprit is traditional sit-ups.

When you do a traditional sit-up, your hip flexors compete with your abs in the first 30 degrees of motion, and beyond that, they take over completely. Since the hip flexors are very strong, they end up doing most of the work, leaving your lower abs relatively undertrained.

Aesthetic considerations aside, a strength imbalance between your lower and upper abdomen can lead to injury. Many lower ab strains occur when the upper abs and hip flexors get tired and the weak lower muscles are unprepared to handle the stress.

Ab Training for the Athlete

Granted that strong abs are vital to good athletic performance, why would athletes need their own special program? Wouldn't the same ab program work for everyone? Well, yes and no. The basic *Legendary Abs* program is the best across-the-board program for abdominal development. But the specific requirements of performance open up the possibility of a few enhancements to make the basic program even more useful to the athlete. Here's why.

SPECIFICITY AND FUNCTIONAL STRENGTH TRAINING

One of the first rules of physical conditioning is the principle of **specificity.** It states that your body adapts very specifically to the demands placed on it. When you do long steady runs, your body responds by developing greater aerobic fitness and endurance. When you do intense heavy lifting, you develop greater strength and muscle mass. Though much research has borne this out, it's really common sense. You wouldn't read a novel to study for a physics test, and you wouldn't hit golf balls to become a better pole vaulter. Your training should mimic the demands of the sport you play.

With this in mind, performance athletes need to do different types of abdominal training than individuals who train solely for appearance. Since sports are dynamic, mobile, and active, athletes must train their muscles to be dynamic, mobile, and active.

Training to meet athletic demands is typically called **functional strength training.** To perform flexing and rotating movements at the level required by most sports means that all your abdominal muscles—upper and lower abs (rectus abdominis) and external and internal obliques—have to be strong. Very strong.

Specifically, functional strength training of the abdomen differs from aesthetic training in three important ways...

FUNCTIONAL TRAINING REQUIREMENTS

1. **Athletes must train for greater upper and lower ab *strength*.** The strength requirements for performance far exceed those for toning and definition. As a consequence of this strength training, athletes will also end up with greater abdominal mass. However, since athletes tend to have bigger muscles overall, their abs will remain in proportion to the rest of their physique.

2. **Athletes need to train the *obliques*.** Most sports involve a significant amount of rotation, or twisting, which is the domain of the oblique muscles.

   In Chapter 1, we recommended you not perform exercises that target the obliques if your main goal is to improve your appearance. This is because the obliques respond quickly to training, and doing exercises that specifically target them—especially weighted side bends or twists—can result in significant oblique development, making you look like you've got a set of "love handles," particularly if you've got any fat in the area to begin with.

   If you're an athlete, though, you *do* need to strengthen your obliques. But that doesn't mean you'll wind up with a pair of unflattering love handles. Most performance athletes have little excess *bodyfat,* which is the real culprit behind love handles. The athlete's oblique muscles themselves, though larger than those of a non-athlete, are balanced by his or her greater muscle mass overall.

3. **Athletes need to train the *hip flexors* in combination with the abdominal muscles.** In Chapter 1, we saw how many so-called abdominal exercises don't work your abs so much as your hip flexors, especially the psoas muscles. Such exercises can put undue stress on the lower spine if done incorrectly. *Athletic performance, however, relies heavily on the hip flexors working in conjunction with the abs.* Running, lifting, jumping, and throwing all bring the hip flexors and abdominals into play simultaneously. (Ever notice the bulging hip flexors of an Olympic sprinter?) So, in order to train specifically for sports performance, you have to train hip flexors and abs together. The trick in doing the exercises that follow is to pay special attention to proper form, and do regular stretching to maintain hip flexor flexibility—this will allow you to train effectively without injury.

About the Athletic Power Program

The basic principles of ab training for performance are similar to those for general abdominal training. You still need to target your abs specifically, force them do more work than normal, and work them from several angles to ensure maximum muscle involvement. The exercises of the *Legendary Abs* program, described in Chapter 3, form the core of the athletic performance program.

In addition, the *Legendary Ab*s Athletic Power Program includes exercises involving rotation and resistance to target the obliques and hip flexors. Second, to meet the functional requirements of athletic performance, it includes a series of dynamic exercises to develop explosive strength.

Athletic Power Program

The routines in the *Legendary Abs Athletic Power Program* contain exercises from the basic *Legendary Abs Program*, described in Chapter 3, *plus* additional exercises that specifically promote rotational strength, as well as strengthen the hip flexors. This chapter describes the new exercises and presents the routines.

ATHLETIC POWER PROGRAM

Hip Flexor Training Precautions

One of the problems with conventional abdominal training is that it's often dangerous. Recall that whenever the stomach muscles tire, there's a tendency to let the lower back arch to accomplish the movement. This focuses the strain on the part of the lower spine where the psoas attach. Arching your back pulls the vertebrae together and can eventually lead to serious back trouble.

Nevertheless, training for athletic performance necessitates doing a certain amount of work to strengthen the hip flexors, including the psoas. How can you train the hip flexors without risking injury?

SEQUENCING

First, as in the basic *Legendary Abs* program, exercise sequence is very important. All hip flexor training and dynamic exercises are done at the beginning of the routine while your abs are still strong and fresh. The goal is to work within the range of movement where both the abs and hip flexors are active, training both sets of muscles simultaneously without straining the back due to fatigued abs.

PRE-EXHAUSTING THE PSOAS

Second, the routines begin with exercises that *isolate* the hip flexors, or psoas, while putting a minimum of stress on the spine. By isolating the hip flexors first, you'll pre-fatigue them before you start exercises that work both hip flexors *and* abs. So while the hip flexors will be relatively tired, your abs will be fresh. This order of exercises lets you train the ab/psoas interaction with the fewest possible number of reps. This will help you to keep your back from arching and hurting your spine.

STRETCHING

Because of the degree to which the hip flexors are worked in these routines, it's very important to stretch them out both before *and* after your ab training routine. The hip flexors can be stretched by doing a Standing Quadriceps Stretch with a slight upward tilt of the pelvis, or a Kneeling Hip Flexor Stretch, which is like a lunge done in a kneeling position. In addition, various hamsting stretches will also stretch the psoas.

"LOCKING IN" THE SPINE FOR STABILITY

Last, exercises that work the abs and hip flexors together require that you learn how to stabilize your spine during exercise. Stabilizing, or "locking in" your spine prevents you from arching your lower back and risking injury. To get an idea of what locking in your spine feels like, purse your lips and blow out fairly hard. You'll feel all your abdominal muscles contract isometrically. That's the feeling you should have when your spine is properly stabilized before an exercise.

Standing Position

To lock in the spine in a standing position, begin by rocking your pelvis back and forth a few times, and then relax. You should now be standing with good posture, and with a very slight curve to your lower back. This is the **neutral position** (Fig. 6-1a). Now lock your spine by tightening your abdomen (Fig. 6-1b). If this is difficult at first, blow out through pursed lips. Then, hold the contraction while continuing to breathe throughout the exercise. It's really quite easy when you get the hang of it.

Fig.6-1a Fig.6-1b

Lying Position

To lock in the spine while lying down, you do what's often called a "pelvic tilt." Rock your pelvis up until your spine flattens along the ground (Fig. 6-2a,b). Then, tighten your stomach muscles. This puts your spine in a good protected position.

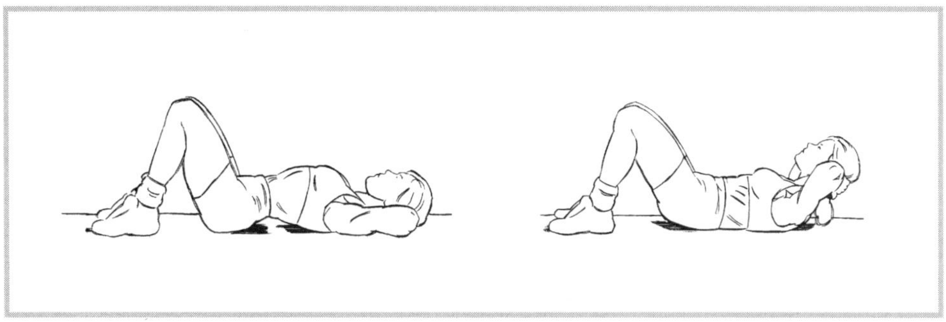

Fig. 6-2a,b

Bent Knee Sit-Ups

STARTING POSITION

Lie flat on the floor and, if possible, anchor your feet or have a training partner hold them in place. Perform a pelvic tilt to stabilize your spine. Now sit up. Begin the exercise from this upright position (Fig. 6-3a).

THE MOVEMENT

Lower yourself until your torso is 30 degrees above the ground (Fig. 6-3b), and then return to upright position. You should feel as if you are pulling from the point where your legs and abdomen meet. Try to maintain the pelvic tilt throughout the exercise.

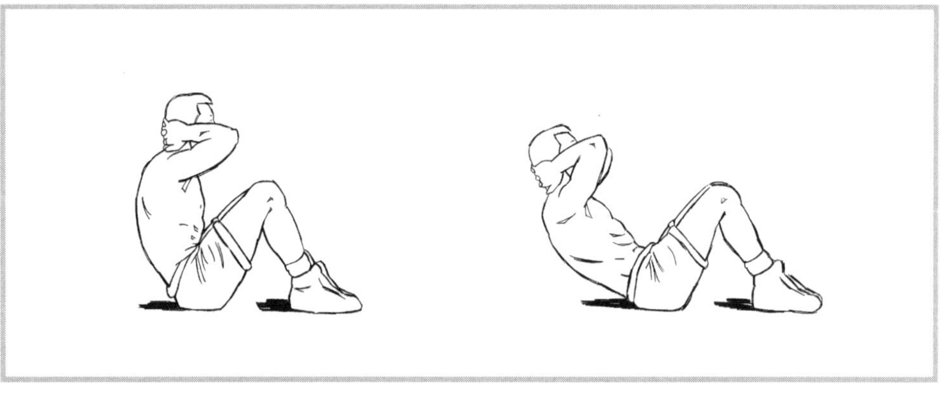

Fig. 6-3a Fig. 6-3b

Lying Knee Pull-Ups

STARTING POSITION

Lie on the floor and stabilize your spine by doing a pelvic tilt. Then extend your arms and hold onto a post or similar fixed object. Bend your legs to form a 90-degree angle at your knees (Fig. 6-4a).

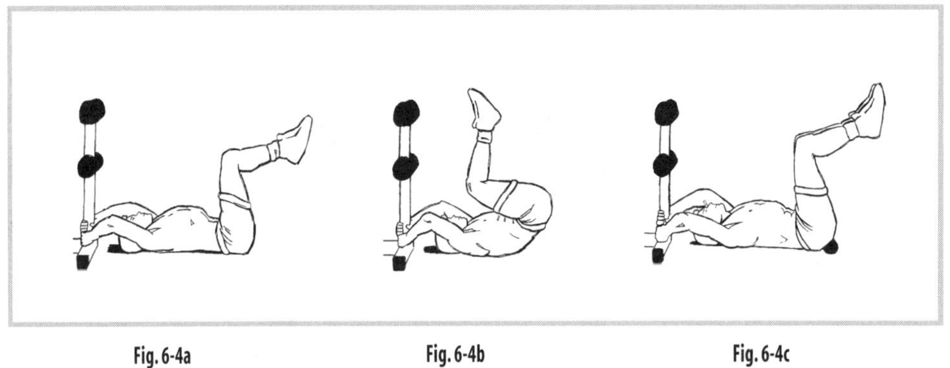

Fig. 6-4a Fig. 6-4b Fig. 6-4c

THE MOVEMENT

Pull your knees toward your chest and return to the starting position. Keep your knees bent at a right angle throughout the movement (Fig. 6-4b). Be sure to maintain the pelvic tilt, and don't arch your back. You might want to put a pad or towel under your buttocks to raise the hips a little (Fig. 6-4c), or use the *Legendary Abs* Crunchbelt. This will help eliminate any arch in your lower back.

Lying Leg Raises

STARTING POSITION

Assume the same position as above, but this time keep your legs almost straight with just a slight bend (Fig. 6-5a).

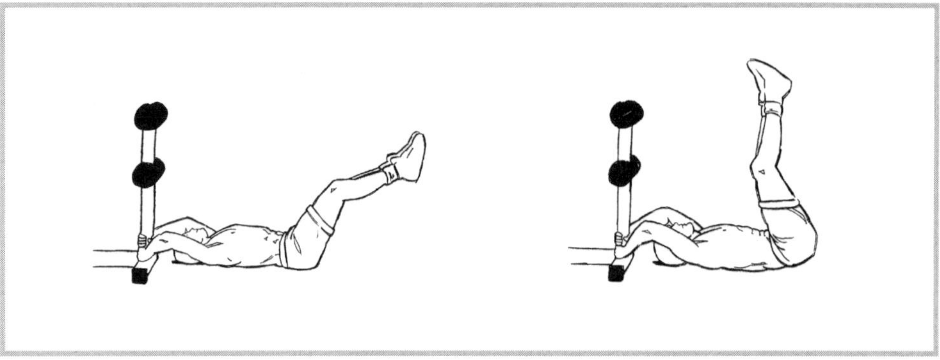

Fig. 6-5a   Fig. 6-5b

THE MOVEMENT

While maintaining a pelvic tilt, raise your legs toward your chest (Fig. 6-5b) and return to the start position. *Note:* This is an advanced exercise and should be done only after you've developed very strong abs and hip flexors. If you can't do this exercise without arching your back, you shouldn't do it at all. Again, placing a pad or towel under your hips can help prevent your back from arching.

Ankle Cable-Pulls

STARTING POSITION

This exercise uses an adjustable weight cable pulley machine. As an alternative, you can use an elastic band of a type that can be attached to your ankle, and anchored to a fixed object at the other end. First, determine the appropriate starting position by extending one leg back about 25 degrees. At that point, the tension on the cable or tubing should be slack. Attach the cable and move to the starting position (Fig. 6-6a). Next, "lock in" your lower spine by contracting your abdomen. Lean slightly forward while keeping the locked position. (It helps to hold on to something for support.)

THE MOVEMENT

Pull your knee forward and up until your thigh is just *slightly* higher than parallel to the ground (Fig. 6-6b). Return your leg slowly to the extended position and repeat. Keep the leg relaxed; don't try to pull your knee by contracting your hamstring muscles. You should feel fatigue only in the hip flexors. Also, make certain that you stay upright with the torso slightly forward.

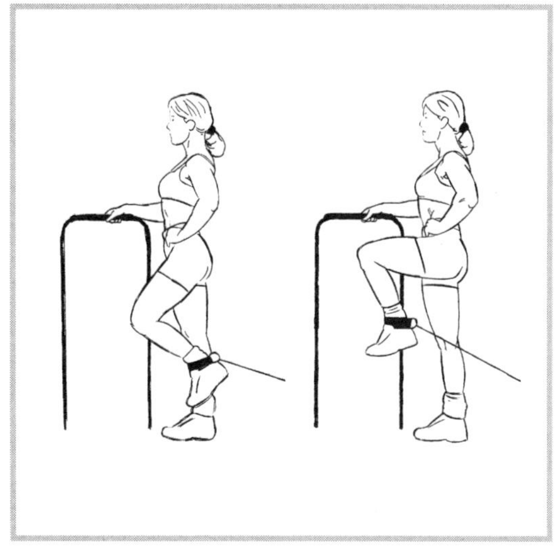

Fig.6-6a Fig.6-6b

In general, don't lean either forward or back. If you have trouble staying in correct position throughout the exercise, decrease the amount of weight or adjust the tension of the tubing.

Note: This exercise takes practice. The tension of the cable or tubing changes with the angle of applied force. Leaning forward *slightly* helps keep the tension constant.

Chop

The next two exercises are often referred to collectively as "Chop and Lift." However, since they are two separate movements that require different set-ups, they will be described separately. Both exercises can be performed with a cable pulley mechanism or with elastic tubing.

STARTING POSITION

Determine your correct starting position by extending your arms in front of you and raising them about 45 degrees. That's where you should grab the cable or tubing to start. Then, turn you body so that you are facing 45 degrees to one side. Step back one-half step with the outside leg and turn the foot out a little to open the hip (Fig. 6-7a). Stabilize your lower spine by slightly contracting your abdomen.

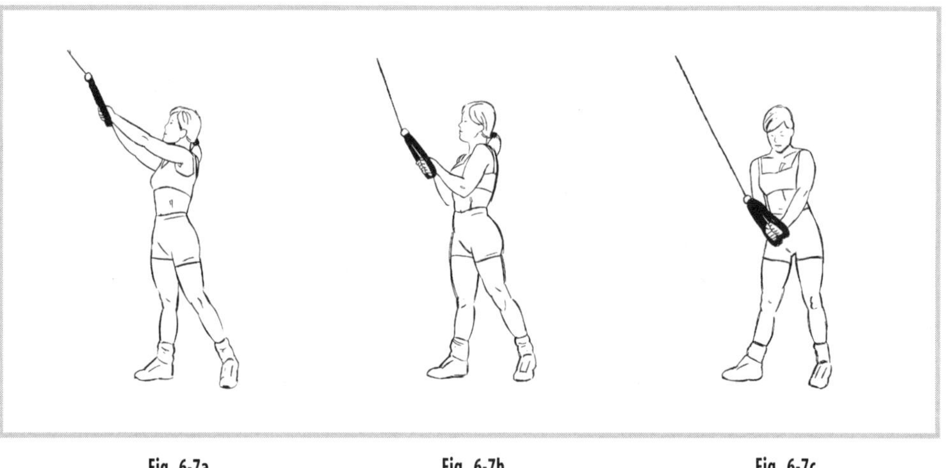

Fig. 6-7a Fig. 6-7b Fig. 6-7c

THE MOVEMENT

Begin the Chop by pulling your elbows down toward your stomach (Fig. 6-7b). When your elbows reach your stomach, continue turning the torso and extend the arms (Fig. 6-7c). Return to the starting position and repeat.

Don't let your hands get ahead of your torso. The torso should turn and the hands should follow. Make sure to keep your torso upright. Done properly, you will feel the exercise on the side to which you are pulling.

When you have completed a set of Chops to one side, switch positions and do the exercise to the other side. *Note:* It is common for one side to be stronger than another. Your goal should be to build balanced strength throughout your torso. You are better off developing both sides equally rather than maximizing strength on one side.

Lift

STARTING POSITION

As you might guess, the Lift is essentially the opposite of the Chop. Fix the cable or tubing so that you start with your hands reaching down and away at a 45-degree angle. Once again, stabilize your torso in an upright position before you begin the Lift. Take one-half step forward and turn the outside foot slightly inward (Fig. 6-8a).

Fig. 6-8a Fig. 6-8b Fig. 6-8c

THE MOVEMENT

Begin the Lift by using your torso to pull your elbows and hands towards your chest (Fig. 6-8b). When your hands reach your chest, keep turning your torso, allowing your feet to pivot slightly, and extend your arms (Fig. 6-8c). Return slowly to starting position.

Note: Don't think of this as a biceps curl with a twist! Use the rotation of your torso—i.e., use your abs—to pull your hands up and forward. The resistance should not be so strong that you are using your biceps to lift the weight. Focus on the movement of your torso. You should feel tension on the side that is opposite your hands in the starting position.

Standing Overhead Tosses

Stand erect with feet even and slightly spread. (As you progress, alternate standing with one foot forward to vary the exercise.) Holding the ball overhead with both hands, bring it behind the head as far as possible in one smooth motion. As you reach back, let the elbows bend a little. Once you feel a stretch of the upper-body muscles, pull forward and throw the ball to a partner, who can then toss it back to you.

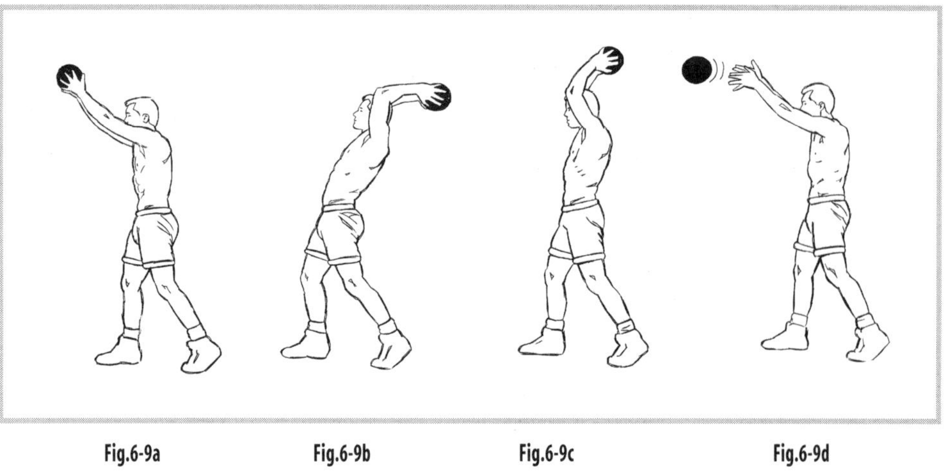

Fig.6-9a Fig.6-9b Fig.6-9c Fig.6-9d

The key to this exercise is quick initiation of the toss. Don't let the ball come to rest as you extend behind your head. On the other hand, don't use a fast jerky wind-up, or you may hurt yourself. Use smooth rhythm reaching back, and then give an explosive toss forward (Fig. 6-9a-d).

Kneeling Overhead Tosses

This exercise is identical to the Standing Toss except that you do it while kneeling (Fig. 6-10 a,b). This further isolates the muscles of the upper body and prevents you from using your legs to generate power.

In the Kneeling Toss, be careful not to bend backwards too far. This can easily happen if you overreach with the ball extended behind your head, and may cause back injury. Remember that the *rate* of stretch is more important than the degree of stretch.

Fig. 6-10a,b

EQUIPMENT NOTE: Medicine Balls

Medicine balls are tremendously effective at building dynamic upper-body strength and explosive power. They come in a range of weights and sizes, and you should choose the ones that seem right for your frame and strength. If anything, choose balls that seem a bit on the light side. Balls that are too heavy will slow the exercise and negate the plyometric effect. Usually, two or three different weighted balls are all you need. (Medicine balls in 2-, 3-, 4-, and 5-kg. weights are available from a number of sports supply companies, including *Health For Life.*)

Twist Tosses

Assume an open stance. Hold the medicine ball in both hands with the arms extended and relaxed. Rotate your upper body, holding the ball in front of your body. Turn until you feel a good stretch, than immediately rotate the upper body forward, throwing the ball. The throw should start from the hips and trunk, with the arms trailing—in effect, you *sling* the ball rather than throw it. Have a partner catch the ball and throw it back (Fig. 6-11a-f).

Fig.6-11a Fig.6-11b Fig.6-11c

Fig. 6-11d Fig. 6-11e Fig. 6-11f

POWER ROUTINES

Athletes training for power should begin by working up through the first 5 levels of the basic *Legendary Abs* program in Chapter 3. *Unlike those training for aesthetics, though, your goal is to advance as quickly as possible.* Once you can do Level 5, jump to the Power Routines listed here. Exercises in the Power Routines that are not described in this chapter are from the basic *Legendary Abs* program, and are described in Chapter 3.

Level 6P

1 Set	**Bent Knee Sit-Ups**	20 reps (m)	*10 sec. rest*
1 Set	**Twist Tosses**	8 reps (m)	*10 sec. rest*
1 Set	**Lying Leg Thrusts**	10 reps (m)	*10 sec. rest*
1 Set	**1/4 Sit-Ups**	20 reps (m)	*10 sec. rest*
1 Set	**Lying Leg Thrusts**	10 reps (m)	*no rest*
1 Set	**1/4 Sit-Ups**	20 reps (m)	*no rest*

Level 7P

1 Set	**Bent Knee Sit-Ups**	25 reps (m)	*10 sec. rest*
1 Set	**Twist Tosses**	10 reps (m)	*10 sec. rest*
1 Set	**Lying Leg Thrusts**	20 reps (m)	*10 sec. rest*
1 Set	**Lying Leg Thrusts**	20 reps (m)	*10 sec. rest*
1 Set	**Ab Crunches**	20 reps (s)	*no rest*
1 Set	**1/4 Sit-Ups**	10 reps (f)	*no rest*

Level 8P

1 Set	**Bent Knee Sit-Ups**	25 reps (m)	*10 sec. rest*
1 Set	**Bent Knee Sit-Ups**	15 reps (m)	*10 sec. rest*
1 Set	**Standing Overhead Tosses**	8 reps (m)	*10 sec. rest*
1 Set	**Twist Tosses**	8 reps (m)	*no rest*
1 Set	**Hanging Knee-Ups**	10 reps (m)	*10 sec. rest*
1 Set	**Hanging Knee-Ups**	8 reps (m)	*10 sec. rest*
1 Set	**Abdominal Crunches**	20 reps (s)	*no rest*
1 Set	**Abdominal Crunches**	20 reps (s)	*no rest*

Level 9P

1 Set	**Ankle Cable Pulls**	8 reps/leg (m)	*no rest*
1 Set	**Bent Knee Sit-Ups**	20 reps (m)	*10 sec. rest*
1 Set	**Bent Knee Sit-Ups**	15 reps (m)	*10 sec. rest*
1 Set	**Kneeling Overhead Tosses**	10 reps (m)	*10 sec. rest*
1 Set	**Twist Tosses**	10 reps (m)	*10 sec. rest*
1 Set	**Hanging Knee-Ups**	15 reps (m)	*10 sec. rest*
1 Set	**Hanging Knee-Ups**	10 reps (m)	*10 sec. rest*
1 Set	**HFL Lying Leg Thrusts**	15 reps (s)	*no rest*
1 Set	**Abdominal Crunches**	20 reps (m)	*no rest*
1 Set	**1/4 Sit-Ups**	10 reps (f)	*no rest*

Level 10P

2 Sets	**Ankle Cable Pulls**	8 reps/leg (m)	*no rest*
1 Set	**Bent Knee Sit-Ups**	20 reps (m)	*10 sec. rest*
1 Set	**Bent Knee Sit-Ups**	15 reps (m)	*10 sec. rest*
1 Set	**Kneeling Overhead Tosses**	10 reps (m)	*no rest*
1 Set	**Twist Tosses**	10 reps (m)	*no rest*
1 Set	**Hanging Knee-Ups**	15 reps (m)	*10 sec. rest*
1 Set	**Hanging Knee-Ups**	15 reps (m)	*10 sec. rest*
1 Set	**HFL Lying Leg Thrusts**	25 reps (s)	*10 sec. rest*
1 Set	**Abdominal Crunches**	25 reps (m)	*no rest*
1 Set	**1/4 Sit-Ups**	10 reps (f)	*no rest*

Level 11P

2 Sets	**Ankle Cable Pulls**	8 reps/leg (m)	*no rest*
1 Set	**Bent Knee Sit-Ups**	20 reps (m)	*10 sec. rest*
1 Set	**Lying Knee Pull-Ups**	10 reps (m)	*10 sec. rest*
1 Set	**Kneeling Overhead Tosses**	10 reps (m)	*no rest*
1 Set	**Chop**	8 reps/side (m)	*10 sec. rest*
1 Set	**Lift**	8 reps/side (m)	*10 sec. rest*
1 Set	**Hanging Knee-Ups**	20 reps (m)	*10 sec. rest*
1 Set	**Hanging Knee-Ups**	15 reps (m)	*10 sec. rest*
1 Set	**HFL Lying Leg Thrusts**	20 reps (s)	*10 sec. rest*
1 Set	**HFL Lying Leg Thrusts**	15 reps (s)	*no rest*
1 Set	**Abdominal Crunches**	30 reps (s)	*no rest*
1 Set	**1/4 Sit-Ups**	15 reps (f)	*no rest*

Level 12P

2 Sets	**Ankle Cable Pulls**	8 reps/leg (m)	*no rest*
1 Set	**Bent Knee Sit-Ups**	25 reps (m)	*10 sec. rest*
1 Set	**Lying Knee Pull-Ups**	15 reps (m)	*10 sec. rest*
1 Set	**Kneeling Overhead Tosses**	10 reps (m)	*no rest*
1 Set	**Twist Tosses**	10 reps (m)	*no rest*
1 Set	**Chop**	8 reps/side (m)	*10 sec. rest*
1 Set	**Lift**	8 reps/side (m)	*10 sec. rest*
1 Set	**Hanging Leg Raises**	5 reps (m)	*10 sec. rest*
1 Set	**Hanging Leg Raises**	5 reps (m)	*10 sec. rest*
1 Set	**Hanging Knee-Ups**	10 reps (m)	*10 sec. rest*
1 Set	**Abdominal Crunches**	35 reps (s)	*no rest*
1 Set	**1/4 Sit-Ups**	15 reps (f)	*no rest*

Level 13P

2 Sets	**Ankle Cable Pulls**	10 reps/leg (m)	*no rest*
1 Set	**Bent Knee Sit-Ups**	35 reps (m)	*10 sec. rest*
2 Sets	**Lying Knee Pull-Ups**	10 reps (m)	*10 sec. rest*
1 Set	**Standing Overhead Throws**	8 reps (m)	*10 sec. rest*
1 Set	**Medicine Ball Twist Tosses**	10 reps (m)	*10 sec. rest*
1 Set	**Chop**	10 reps/side (m)	*10 sec. rest*
1 Set	**Lift**	10 reps/side (m)	*10 sec. rest*
1 Set	**Hanging Leg Raises**	10 reps (m)	*10 sec. rest*
3 Sets	**Hanging Knee-Ups**	5 reps (m)	*10 sec. rest*
1 Set	**Lying Leg Thrusts**	20 reps (m)	*no rest*
1 Set	**Abdominal Crunches**	30 reps (s)	*no rest*
1 Set	**1/4 Sit-Ups**	15 reps (f)	*no rest*

Level 14P

2 Sets	**Ankle Cable Pulls**	10 reps/leg (m)	*no rest*
2 Sets	**Bent Knee Sit-Ups**	20 reps (m)	*10 sec. rest*
1 Set	**Lying Knee Pull-Ups**	10 reps (m)	*10 sec. rest*
1 Set	**Lying Leg Raises**	5 reps (m)	*10 sec. rest*
1 Set	**Standing Overhead Tosses**	10 reps (m)	*10 sec. rest*
1 Set	**Kneeling Overhead Tosses**	10 reps (m)	*10 sec. rest*
1 Set	**Twist Tosses**	10 reps (m)	*10 sec. rest*
2 Sets	**Chop**	8 reps/side (m)	*10 sec. rest*
2 Sets	**Lift**	8 reps/side (m)	*10 sec. rest*
2 Sets	**Hanging Leg Raises**	5 reps (m)	*10 sec. rest*
2 Sets	**Hanging Knee-Ups**	5 reps (m)	*10 sec. rest*
1 Set	**Lying Leg Thrusts**	20 reps (m)	*10 sec. rest*
1 Set	**Lying Leg Thrusts**	15 reps (m)	*10 sec. rest*
1 Set	**Abdominal Crunches**	30 reps (s)	*no rest*
1 Set	**1/4 Sit-Ups**	15 reps (f)	*no rest*
1 Set	**Knee Rock-Backs**	10 reps (m)	*no rest*

Level 15P

2 Sets	**Ankle Cable Pulls**	10 reps/leg (m)	*no rest*
2 Sets	**Bent Knee Sit-Ups**	25 reps (m)	*10 sec. rest*
1 Set	**Lying Leg Raises**	10 reps (m)	*10 sec. rest*
2 Sets	**Kneeling Overhead Tosses**	10 reps (m	*10 sec. rest*)
1 Set	**Twist Tosses**	10 reps (m)	*10 sec. rest*
2 Sets	**Chop**	10 reps/side (m)	*10 sec. rest*
2 Sets	**Lift**	10 reps/side (m)	*10 sec. rest*
2 Sets	**Hanging Leg Raises**	10 reps (m)	*10 sec. rest*
2 Sets	**Hanging Knee-Ups**	10 reps (m)	*10 sec. rest*
2 Sets	**Lying Leg Thrusts**	10 reps (m)	*10 sec. rest*
1 Set	**Cross-Knee Ab Crunches**	15 reps (s)	*10 sec. rest*
1 Set	**Abdominal Crunches**	30 reps (s)	*no rest*
1 Set	**1/4 Sit-Ups**	15 reps (f)	*no rest*
1 Set	**Knee Rock-Backs**	15 reps (m)	*no rest*

THE SCHEDULE

The *Legendary Abs* Athletic Power Routines are intended for athletes who already have a basic level of abdominal conditioning. Even if you are quite active in your sport, you should begin your ab training by working up through the first 5 levels of the basic *Legendary Abs* program in Chapter 3, *advancing as quickly as possible.* As soon as you can meet the rep goals for a particular level, move up to the next.

Once you can do Level 5 of the basic program, jump to level 6P in the Power Routines, and continue up through all the Power levels. Here again, push yourself to advance as quickly as you can. A good average rate of advancement is about one level every three weeks.

As mentioned earlier, be sure to stretch before and after your ab workout.

Appendix A

Q & A: Answers to Frequently-Asked Training Questions

In the 15-plus years since the first edition of *Legendary Abs*, we've received hundreds of letters from readers. Besides a huge amount of praise for the program, these have often contained helpful comments and suggestions, many of which we have incorporated into subsequent editions. We've also received our share of questions. In this chapter, we share answers to some those most frequently asked.

Questions & Answers

Q These seem like pretty standard exercises—in fact, I'm already doing some of them. What's so special about this program?

A There's no comparison between doing the *Legendary Abs* routines, and doing *some* of the same exercises haphazardly. As explained in Chapter 1, you experience a dramatic increase in the efficiency of an abdominal routine—or any routine—if the interdependency of the muscle groups is taken into consideration. *Legendary Abs* will accomplish what a random approach never will, and will do it in the shortest time possible. The best way to convince yourself of this, though, is to try it.

Q I already work out five times a week and spend 20 minutes at each workout doing abs. How can 6 minutes of exercise equal that?

A Synergism! See Chapter 1.

Q I don't have any place to do the hanging exercises. What can I do?

A You have several options. The least expensive is to purchase a doorway-mounted chinning bar, available from most sporting goods stores. Be sure to get the kind with metal brackets that screw into the door frame to prevent the bar from coming loose while you're hanging. The only disadvantage of this type of bar is that unless you have a very tall doorway, you have to keep your knees bent so your feet don't drag.

A better choice if you have the space is a free-standing device like the Gold's Gym Power Tower. This is a tall, relatively lightweight steel frame designed to accommodate a variety of exercises, including Pull-Ups, Leg-Raises, elevated Push-Ups, and Triceps Dips, among others.

The third option is to build your own. If you need help, Health For Life publishes a manual of 3 different hanging bar plans of varying complexity for do-it-yourselfers of all skill levels. [Chinning Bar Plans or Power Tower are also available from Health For Life, at 1-800-874-5339].

Q **If there's no place I can set up a chinning bar, can I substitute some other exercise for Hanging Leg Raises?**

A Unfortunately, any substitution is a bit of a compromise. No other exercise creates such ideally poor leverage for the lower abs while at the same time guarding your lower back against arching.

However, if no chinning bar is available, the next best alternative is the hanging chair found on many Universal machines (not to be confused with a Roman Chair, which is *not* recommended). The drawback of using this chair is that it encourages your lower back to arch. You'll have to work hard to keep your pelvis tilted up throughout the exercise. Doing leg raises with an arched back is worse than doing no lower ab exercise at all.

Only if finding a suitable place to hang is impossible should you make the following modification to the program:

- Substitute an extra set of HFL Lying Leg Thrusts, according to the table below. This extra set should be done first, in place of all hanging sets on a given level.

- Skip program levels 2 through 4. In other words, when you are ready to move up from Level 1, go directly to Level 5. Levels 2 through 4 are designed to prepare you for Hanging Leg Raises and therefore won't be useful to you. For the same reason, skip Level 6.

Substituting HFL Lying Leg Thrusts for all sets of hanging exercises

LEVEL 5	Substitute 1 set, 25 reps
LEVEL 7	Substitute 1 set, 30 reps
LEVEL 8	Substitute 1 set, 30 reps
LEVEL 9	Substitute 1 set, 30 reps

Q **Why do my lower abs seem to develop slower than my upper abs?**

A Because in lower ab training it is easier to unconsciously cheat! The psoas muscles perform movements similar to those of the lower abs, and if leg raises are done without attention to form, the psoas can end up doing most or all of the work. Lower abs are not slower to develop than upper abs, they are simply more difficult to focus on.

Q **Hanging and Lying Leg Raises (or Leg Thrusts) make my back hurt.**

A This often happens if the psoas become over involved. Since the psoas muscles are anchored to your lumbar vertebrae and hoist your legs by tugging on the spine, doing Leg Raises incorrectly—using the psoas instead of the abs—can induce lower back pain and over time may cause injury.

Always pay strict attention to form. If your lower back arches at all, your psoas muscles are dominating the movement. As long as your back remains flat or rounded, you can be fairly sure your abs are the prime mover.

Q **Some of the routines show an exercise called Pull-Down Ab Crunches. What if I don't have the lat pull-down bar necessary for doing this exercise?**

A The Pull-Down Ab Crunch is an optional exercise. It's included as a way for bodybuilders or other serious athletes to train using progressive resistance for greater development. An alternate way of doing this exercise is by grasping both ends of an elastic band slung over your chinning bar, and performing the exercise as shown in Chapter 3, using the band's resistance. *(Always use caution when training with an elastic band!)*

Q **How do I know when it's time to move up to the next level of the routines?**

A In the basic *Legendary Abs* program (Chapter 3) there are no bonus points for moving up to the higher levels! Your goal should be to stay on each level as long as possible, using focus and intensity to get the most out of it. As long as you're seeing results on a level, stay there. When you think it's really getting too easy, take the appropriate self-evaluation test in Appendix B. On the other hand, if you're doing the Athletic Power Routines in Chapter 6, the reverse is true: Athletes are trying to build endurance, and should therefore advance through the levels as quickly as possible.

Q **I'm not feeling a burn after doing hanging exercises. Does this mean I'm doing them wrong—or is it time to move to the next level?**

A Probably neither. The routines are designed to generate a cumulative fatigue level, leaving you with a burn at the end of the routine—not in the middle. If you're able to get through the whole routine without a burn, check for correct form and then take the appropriate self-evaluation test in Appendix B. It may be time to move up.

Q **Should I do *Legendary Abs* before or after cardio work?**

A If you're doing a long aerobic workout involving a certain amount of muscle conditioning or calisthenics, do *Legendary Abs* first. Otherwise, use aerobic activity like running, swimming, cycling, stair climbing, or jumping rope as a warm-up for the ab routines.

Q **Will *Legendary Abs* help me lose my love handles?**

A *Legendary Abs* will firm and tone your abdominal muscles. Getting rid of love handles, however, means losing excess fat. These are separate processes, but they can be done at the same time. For complete instructions on bodyfat reduction, see Chapter 4, and give the *Legendary Abs* High-Low plan a try.

Q **Are side bends a good exercise for slimming your waist? What about side bends with weights?**

A If you're doing side bends, especially with weights—stop! As explained in Chapter 1, you can't burn fat doing abdominal exercise. Weighted side bends will simply build up the oblique muscles beneath the fat, giving you even larger, firmer love handles. Ab machines that train the obliques using rotational movements will have the same effect.

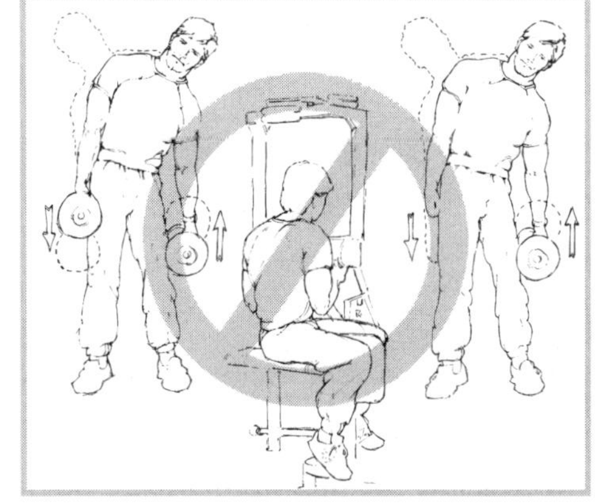

Side bends and rotational ab machines tend to produce overdeveloped external obliques—they are not effective ways to slim your waist.

Q What about seated twists? Are they worthwhile?

A Seated twists fall into a category with other ab, waist, and lower back calisthenic exercises that attempt to tone muscle while also burning fat. As explained in Chapter 1, these are two separate goals, each requiring its own type of training. Fat loss is best accomplished by combining aerobic exercise with proper nutrition to get your body burning more calories than it takes in. For building abdominal muscle, of course, there's nothing more effective than *Legendary Abs*.

Twists are neither an effective abdominal toning exercise, nor an effective aerobic exercise.

Q Can I do the routines every day? How about twice a day?

A In the case of abdominal training, more is not better. Doing the program twice a day, or five times a week, or with higher numbers of reps than specified will not increase your rate of progress. In fact, any of those can lead to diminished results due to insufficient recovery time for the ab muscles.

What's important is to give the program all you've got during those few minutes you devote to it. Then relax and let your body do the rest. Remember, muscles grow while resting, not while exerting!

Q If I'm training for increased size, how do I incorporate weights into the program?

A Weights ranging from 1 to 25 pounds may be used during several exercises:

- Crunches and Cross-Knee Crunches (weight held behind the head)
- Hanging and Lying Leg Raises or Leg Thrusts (using ankle weights)

Pull-Down Ab Crunches, of course, always involve weight. It will probably also involve considerably more than 25 pounds.

When training for size, follow the standard rep guidelines for overload: 6 to 8 reps per set. This means you will ignore the rep numbers listed in the program for the particular exercises you add weight to.

If you are training for definition and not size, you may still wish to use small amounts of weight during some of these exercises, while maintaining the higher rep numbers specified in the routines. Only if you are interested in gaining size should you progressively increase the amount of weight used. Even then, be aware that small increases in weight will make a big difference. If you have a wide variety of plates, move up by the smallest increment possible—ideally, 1 to 3 pounds at a time.

Appendix B Self-Evaluation

At some point, you may find that you've mastered parts of the level you're on and are still struggling with other parts of it. How can you tell whether it's time to move up to the next level? If you're doing the Athletic Power Routines in Chapter 6, you should move up as soon as you can reach the rep goals. For those doing the basic *Legendary Abs* program, though, the decision to move up must be based largely on a subjective assessment of your overall progress and results. This simple test will help you make that assessment.

Instructions

Go to the test page corresponding to the level you're on. Perform the routine. Fill in the number of reps you're able to do for each exercise. If your rep number for an exercise falls within the goal range for that exercise, put a check in the ACHIEVED box. Figure out the total number of reps you performed in the entire routine and enter that number at the bottom of the column.

To pass the test, you must have checked all of the ACHIEVED boxes, and your rep total must be above the REP GOAL listed for TOTAL REPS. The instructions at the end of the test will help you determine whether you've passed.

In case you need to take the test for a particular level more than once, each test grid has three columns for additional trials.

SAMPLE LEVEL

Write in the numbers of reps you do when you take the test.

Check here if number of reps done is within the range specified in the "Rep Goal" column.

Exercise	Trial 1	Trial 2	Trial 3	Trial 4	Rep Goal	Achieved
HFL Lying Leg Thrusts	19				1 set / 15 reps	✓
1/4 Sit-Ups	24				1 set / 25 reps	
Total Reps:	43				44 reps	no

Total all reps done for this level and enter total here.

Check here if Total Reps done is equal to or greater than the goal specified in the "Rep Goal" column.

If you haven't passed, don't be discouraged! Passing the test isn't the idea—getting results is. Not passing means you're still making progress, and you don't have to move up to a harder level yet.

If you do pass the test, ask yourself: *Am I still getting results?* If the answer is yes, continue on the same level as before. Only if you feel you are no longer getting results should you move up. Remember, there's no reason to work harder when you can get the same results with less work!

The Tests

LEVEL A

Exercise	Trial 1	Trial 2	Trial 3	Trial 4	Rep Goal	Achieved
HFL Lying Leg Thrusts					14-15 reps	
1/4 Sit-Ups					23-25 reps	
HFL Lying Leg Thrusts					7-10 reps	
1/4 Sit-Ups					17-20 reps	
Total Reps:					**65 reps**	

If you have checked all the ACHIEVED boxes *and* you are no longer getting results, move up to Level 1.

LEVEL 1

Exercise	Trial 1	Trial 2	Trial 3	Trial 4	Rep Goal	Achieved
HFL Lying Leg Thrusts					23-25 reps	
HFL Lying Leg Thrusts					17-20 reps	
Abdominal Crunches					24-25 reps	
1/4 Sit-Ups					8-10 reps	
Total Reps:					**76 reps**	

If you have checked all the ACHIEVED boxes *and* you are no longer getting results, move up to Level 2.

LEVEL 2

Exercise	Trial 1	Trial 2	Trial 3	Trial 4	Rep Goal	Achieved
Hanging Knee-Ups					9-10 reps	
Hanging Knee-Ups					6-8 reps	
Abdominal Crunches					24-25 reps	
Abdominal Crunches					17-20 reps	
Total Reps:					**59 reps**	

If you have checked all the ACHIEVED boxes *and* you are no longer getting results, move up to Level 3.

LEVEL 3

Exercise	Trial 1	Trial 2	Trial 3	Trial 4	Rep Goal	Achieved
Hanging Knee-Ups					14-15 reps	
Hanging Knee-Ups					8-10 reps	
HFL Lying Leg Thrusts					14-15 reps	
Abdominal Crunches					19-20 reps	
1/4 Sit-Ups					8-10 reps	
Total Reps:					**66 reps**	

If you have checked all the ACHIEVED boxes *and* you are no longer getting results, move up to Level 4.

LEVEL 4

Exercise	Trial 1	Trial 2	Trial 3	Trial 4	Rep Goal	Achieved
Hanging Knee-Ups					19 -20 reps	
Hanging Knee-Ups					13 -15 reps	
HFL Lying Leg Thrusts					19 -20 reps	
HFL Lying Leg Thrusts					13 -15 reps	
Abdominal Crunches					27 -30 reps	
1/4 Sit-Ups					8 -10 reps	
Total Reps:					**104 reps**	

If you have checked all the ACHIEVED boxes *and* you are no longer getting results, move up to Level 5.

LEVEL 5

Exercise	Trial 1	Trial 2	Trial 3	Trial 4	Rep Goal	Achieved
Hanging Knee-Ups					24 -25 reps	
Hanging Knee-Ups					17 -20 reps	
HFL Lying Leg Thrusts					19 -20 reps	
HFL Lying Leg Thrusts					13 -15 reps	
Abdominal Crunches					30 -35 reps	
1/4 Sit-Ups					13-15 reps	
Total Reps:					**124 reps**	

If you have checked all the ACHIEVED boxes *and* you are no longer getting results, move up to Level 6.

LEVEL 6

Exercise	Trial 1	Trial 2	Trial 3	Trial 4	Rep Goal	Achieved
Hanging Leg Raises					5 reps	
Hanging Leg Raises					4 - 5 reps	
Hanging Knee-Ups					9 -10 reps	
Abdominal Crunches					33 -35 reps	
1/4 Sit-Ups					12 -15 reps	
Total Reps:					**66 reps**	

If you have checked all the ACHIEVED boxes *and* you are no longer getting results, move up to Level 7.

LEVEL 7

Exercise	Trial 1	Trial 2	Trial 3	Trial 4	Rep Goal	Achieved
Hanging Leg Raises					9 -10 reps	
Hanging Knee-Ups					5 reps	
Hanging Leg Raises					5 reps	
Hanging Knee-Ups					4 - 5 reps	
HFL Lying Leg Thrusts					22 -25 reps	
Abdominal Crunches					33 -35 reps	
1/4 Sit-Ups					12 -15 reps	
Total Reps:					**95 reps**	

If you have checked all the ACHIEVED boxes *and* you are no longer getting results, move up to Level 8.

SELF-EVALUATION

LEVEL 8

Exercise	Trial 1	Trial 2	Trial 3	Trial 4	Rep Goal	Achieved
Hanging Leg Raises					9 -10 reps	
Hanging Knee-Ups					4 -5 reps	
Hanging Leg Raises					8 -10 reps	
Hanging Knee-Ups					4 -5 reps	
HFL Lying Leg Thrusts					29 -30 reps	
HFL Lying Leg Thrusts					22 -25 reps	
Abdominal Crunches					35 reps	
1/4 Sit-Ups					13 -15 reps	
Knee Rock-Backs					15 reps	
Total Reps:					**146 reps**	

If you have checked all the ACHIEVED boxes *and* you are no longer getting results, move up to Level 9.

B

SELF-EVALUATION

SOME OF OUR OTHER COURSES:

THE HUMAN FUEL HANDBOOK

Health For Life's guide to peak performance nutrition, written especially for the dedicated athlete. Nutrient by nutrient, you'll discover how protein, carbohydrate, fat, minerals and vitamins function in your body...and why much of what you've heard about these substances is wrong. You'll get the real story on energy production, sports drinks, free-form amino acids, B-15, ginseng, Omega-3, steroid replacements, and much more! *Over 300 pages.*

SECRETS OF ADVANCED BODYBUILDERS

What Legendary Abs does for abdominal conditioning, **Secrets of Advanced Bodybuilders** does for your whole workout! **Secrets** explains how to apply the Synergism Principle to training back, chest, delts, biceps, triceps, quads, and hamstrings. It unlocks the secrets of the Optimum Workout and shows you how to develop the best routines for you—with your particular goals, strengths, and body structure.

Get the ultimate program. Plus, learn...A new back exercise that will pile on the mass and increase power without putting harmful stress on your lower back • A technique for making Leg Extensions 200% more intense by targeting both inner and outer quads • The shift in position that cranks pull-up and pull-down exercises to three times normal intensity • A body weight triceps exercise that will be "a growing experience" even for someone who's been training for years • A body weight lat exercise that will mass up your back faster than you would have believed possible • A special shoulder set that's more effective than most entire delt routines —also— The best way to integrate your other athletic endeavors—running, cycling, stretching, mountain climbing, martial arts, etc.—into your routine to create the optimum overall program • Techniques for maximizing the effectiveness of all exercises you do, not just those in the course...and much, much more! Stop working harder than you need to to get the results you want. Put the **Secrets of Advanced Bodybuilders** to work for you today! *158 pp. Over 300 illustrations.*

MIND GAINS

Health For Life brings you a new, effective way to master the psychological tools of peak performance. Based on the techniques which led Eastern Bloc athletes to gold medal after gold medal, combined with the latest in Western sports psychology, **Mind Gains** is your ticket to the last frontier of physical performance.

You'll learn: How to cope with performance anxiety • How to stay motivated to succeed despite injuries, boredom, and other obstacles • How low self-esteem can sabotage your performance, and what you can do about it• How to achieve what psychologists call optimal arousal, a state in which time seems to slow and perfect technique execution occurs with ease • How to tell negative inner voices to shut up.

From proper goal setting to mental imagery rehearsals, you'll discover a wealth of new resources to increase your performance, gains, and personal satisfaction. Get the mental edge with **Mind Gains**! *150 pp., illustrated.*

TRANSFIGURE I: FOR THE ULTIMATE BUTTOCKS AND THIGHS

Transfigure I is a revolutionary, high-gear system of buttock and thigh conditioning, keyed to a woman's specific aesthetic goals and based on sound biomechanical principles. Forget doing hundreds of ineffective leg exercises. Get set for the fastest results you've ever experienced, with routines that allow you to take control of your body and create the lean, shapely form you want! **Transfigure I** includes separate routines involving body weight exercise, light resistance exercise—even competition bodybuilding work. Whether you're working for general firmness and tone, or strength and high definition, **Transfigure I** is your formula for the ultimate lower body, in just 9 minutes! *126 pp. Over 200 photographs.*

TRANSFIGURE II: FOR THE ULTIMATE UPPER BODY

Part two of our body-sculpting program for women, **Transfigure II** adds the finishing touches to the ultimate physique. It concentrates on two areas that make the biggest difference in the shape and definition of the upper body: the backs of the upper arms and the chest. It also promotes attractive, balanced development of the shoulders, back and biceps. From light-resistance exercises all the way to competition bodybuilding work...you select the intensity that matches your experience and goals. For all-around firmness, tone and shapely definition. *130 pp. Over 100 photographs.*

SYNERSHAPE: A SCIENTIFIC WEIGHT LOSS GUIDE

We're surrounded by weight loss myths. Crash diets. Spot reducing. Exotic herbs. Still, most plans fail, and most people who lose weight gain it back again. Is there really an honest, effective solution? Yes! **SynerShape** represents the next generation in awareness of how the body gains and metabolizes fat. It synthesizes the most recent findings on nutrition, exercise, and psychology into a TOTAL program, offering you the tools you need to shape the body you want. **SynerShape** works. Let it work for you! *24 pp. illustrated manual.*

THE PSYCHOLOGY OF WEIGHT LOSS

This special program-on-tape picks up where **SynerShape** leaves off. Noted psychologist Carol Landesman explores eating problems and solutions based on the latest research into human behavior and metabolism. Then, through a series of exercises, she helps you begin to heal the emotional conflicts behind your weight problem. **The Psychology of Weight Loss** is a unique program that brings the power of the therapy process into the privacy of your home. *A 90-minute guided introspection. On audio cassette.*

MAX 0_2: THE COMPLETE GUIDE TO SYNERGISTIC AEROBIC TRAINING

Maximize your aerobic capacity faster and with less work than ever before! **Max 0_2** represents an exciting new breakthrough in aerobic training. It offers a completely new perspective on the combined effect of VO_2 max and lactate threshold—and on the vital role this effect plays in optimum aerobic conditioning.

Learn: How the F.I.T. principle (Frequency, Intensity, and Time) can help you experience the same progress in your cardiovascular training as in other parts of your workout • How to build aerobics into any conditioning program (Bodybuilders: here's the secret to dropping bodyfat without losing muscle mass!) • Benefits and myths of cross-training • How to avoid injuries that can be caused by high-intensity aerobic work • Losing weight • Endurance events • and much, much more! *Over 200 pp., illustrated.*

THE 7-MINUTE ROTATOR CUFF SOLUTION

Almost everyone who works out experiences some kind of rotator cuff injury during a lifetime of training. Any of these injuries could spell the end of a workout career, but most can be prevented. **The 7-Minute Rotator Cuff Solution** is a quick, simple program to help prevent (or help you recover from) rotator cuff injuries. It explains in detail how the shoulder works, what can go wrong and why, and exactly what to do (and not to do) to stop shoulder problems before they happen. Plus: a simple 7-minute exercise program that can eliminate shoulder pain and restore normal shoulder function in just a few weeks. *144 pp., illustrated.*

SYNERSTRETCH: FOR TOTAL BODY FLEXIBILITY...FAST!

Two programs in one. Both deliver lower- and upper-body flexibility in less than 8 minutes a day! **SynerStretch A** is for you if you need to maintain your flexibility. Originally designed for martial artists, who depend on extreme flexibility, **SynerStretch A** will also help bodybuilders, dancers, and other athletes stay flexible in less than 5 minutes per workout. A great way to end a training session of any kind! **SynerStretch B** is for you if you need to increase your flexibility. Not only does it take less than 8 minutes, but because it makes use of a new, relatively unknown technique (Isometric Agonist Contraction/Relaxation), it eliminates most of the pain usually associated with stretching. It works! When you order **SynerStretch**, you get both programs in one manual. Get loose, and stay loose with **SynerStretch**. *28 pp., illustrated manual. Also available on video.*

POWER FOREARMS!

Here at last is a program that specifically targets the hard-to-develop forearm muscles. Like all Health For Life programs, **Power ForeArms!** is based on the Synergism principle and yields maximum results in minimum time. Designed for serious bodybuilders and martial artists, Power ForeArms! will help you build strong, solid, massive forearms in just 7 to 12 minutes, twice a week. Give **Power ForeArms!** a try. *32 pp., illustrated manual. Also available on video.*